7 SECRETS

TO

SUCCESS

7 SPECIFIC STRATEGIES I USED TO OVERCOME
5 YEARS OF FAILURE IN DIRECT SELLING

By
Matt Morris

© 2020 Matt Morris

Success Publishing, LLC
P.O. Box 703536
Dallas TX 75370
United States
questions@mattmorris.com

ISBN: 978-1-970073-41-6

Contents

The Only Difference
Between You and Me

First and foremost, I want to start by congratulating you on taking the time out of your busy schedule to sit down and commit to reading this book. By making the choice to embark on the journey towards understanding and applying the 7 Secrets to Success, you're taking the first step towards changing the rest of your life in incredible ways.

And by taking that step, you're putting yourself well ahead of the game by doing something that the majority of people never even think to do—investing in yourself. There are so many people out there who don't bat an eye at spending hundreds or even thousands of dollars a year on fuel for their car, but balk at the prospect of investing that same amount of money into fuel for the most valuable and precious possession: their mind.

The late Jim Rohn, a successful entrepreneur, author, and legendary speaker, said that, "formal education will make you a living, but self-education will make you a fortune." By picking up this book, by dedicating the focused time and energy needed to study and apply the principles and strategies outlined in it, you are choosing to make that investment, to educate yourself, to further your understanding, and to begin bringing the life of your dreams into reality.

You may not know it yet, but you're beginning down a path that will lead you to experience a level of success and abundance that will exceed your wildest expectations and blow away all notions of what you thought was possible for your life.

How do I know this? Because I've lived it. It seems like only yesterday that I was thirty-thousand dollars in debt, homeless, and living out of my little, red, beat-up Honda Civic.

Sounds bad enough already, right? Well how about the fact that I was, and I kid you not, bathing in gas station bathrooms while attempting to make a living selling above-ground swimming pools door-to-door during the hottest two months of the summer.

Rock bottom? Yeah, she was once a close personal friend of mine. But it was during this time in my life that I experienced the kind of come-to-Jesus moment that I think we all become familiar with at least a few times throughout our lives. Mine was a little more literal however, considering I was in the parking lot of a church when it happened.

I found myself in a little town on the other side of Louisiana, with a meeting scheduled to (hopefully) sell someone on the joys and splendor that an above-ground swimming pool could bring to their life. I had driven across the state that night just so I could make the appointment by morning, praying it would go well because I was painfully aware of how badly I needed a sale.

The only problem? I was also painfully aware of how long it had been since my last gas station bath, and I knew a severe case of B.O. wasn't going to help me sell anything to anyone. I drove around the one-stoplight town looking for a place to bathe, but of course the only gas station in town was already closed.

So I drove around in the pouring rain a little longer until I finally came across my preferred sleeping spot: a church parking lot. It admittedly gave me a small sense of security. After all, a would-be car-jacker would probably feel at least a little guilty committing grand theft auto at a church, right?

With my doors locked, I leaned my seat back and settled in to get some much-needed shut eye. There was only one problem: I couldn't sleep. The reason? *Because I could almost taste how bad I smelled.* Do you know how rank you have to be before you finally get grossed out by your own scent?

I'm thinking to myself, *"No way I'm going to sell anything going into their house smelling like this."*

What to do? Well, I saw the rain and I saw an empty parking lot and I thought to myself, *"Why not?"*

I stripped down to nothing, grabbed my bar of soap, and started showering in the rain. If you've ever had to do this out of necessity, and I hope you've never had to, then you'll know that the water pressure of rain is, well, not great... and it certainly doesn't compare to being under a showerhead.

So, there I was, butt-naked in the middle of a church parking lot, trying to wash the soap off me, wondering if it's only a matter of time before someone driving by on the main road next to the church decides to have me arrested for indecent exposure.

That's when I noticed a gutter off the side of the church with a little more concentrated water pressure than the rain. Yes, you guessed it, I rinsed myself off in the *gutter run-off* before drying myself and getting back in my car.

Rock bottom? I think I had just made her my girlfriend. That was the moment I realized that I had sunk as low as I could possibly go with no real idea of how I was going to pull myself out.

There are two great motivators in life: the desire for pleasure and the avoidance of pain. Which one is greater? You got it - pain.

That night I spent in small-town Louisiana was a turning point. It was in the gutter run-off of that church parking lot where a burning desire to make real, lasting change welled up inside of me.

It was where I finally snapped out of my half-sleep state of mediocrity, where I woke up declaring "enough is enough." As a result, much like many of you will have by reading this book, I had an awakening.

I had read this article on the human body saying that every 7 years, every cell in your body dies and is re-generated. And based on what you feed your cells (food, nutrition, water, etc), you can re-invent your level of health.

I thought, *"If you can re-invent your body, surely I can re-invent my level of success."*

That began what I call my re-invention process. I began ferociously looking for the principles and strategies that could turn my life around.

Over the next few years, that's exactly what happened. I was able to completely reinvent who I was and elevate my quality of life. Between the ages of twenty-one to twenty-four, I went from being homeless, broke, and living out of my car, to earning a six-figure income working for myself, taking exotic vacations around the world, and living my dream life.

By the time I was twenty-nine, I was a millionaire helping several others to earn six-figure incomes. Since then, I've personally earned well over eight figures, generated over a billion dollars in revenues throughout my sales organizations, and have helped over 50 people from all over the world become million-dollar earners creating freedom, abundance, and wealth for themselves.

If those are the kind of results you're looking for, and more importantly are committed to achieving, get excited because what you're about to learn are the seven specific strategies I used to make that a reality.

Why am I telling you these success stories? I promise you it isn't out of ego or because I think I'm better than anyone else. In fact, it's the exact opposite; I'm telling you this because *I am no different than you.*

I was never the brightest or the best in school. I struggled immensely when I first got started in business. There are no God-given gifts or talents that set me that far apart from anyone else in the world.

The success I've experienced is because of one thing and one thing only: the absolute mastery and daily implementation of these strategies, to the point where they have become as natural to me as breathing.

So much so, that you could drop me in any major city in the world, without any of my contacts or resources, and with one-hundred-percent certainty I know I could become a millionaire within twelve to twenty-four months. That's how strong my confidence is both in myself and in these principles. My goal and intention for you is that you will grow to believe in yourself and your abilities just as greatly.

Right now? The only difference between you and me is my understanding of the 7 Secrets.

And luckily for you, you don't have to learn it alone the way I did. My purpose for writing this book is to give you a shortcut to success. And when I say shortcut, please don't get me wrong. I'm not talking about cutting corners or saying that you don't have to work amazingly hard. You do. What I'm referring to is doing the right work based on the right principles.

When I got started as an entrepreneur, I was willing to do the work. I just didn't have the proper direction so I focused on things that didn't matter and it took me years longer than it should have. I wish I would have had this book so I could have directed my energies in the proper way.

If you're anything like me - and since you picked up this book I'll go ahead and assume that you are - you have an enormous desire to create a seven-figure income for yourself. You have a fire in your belly driving you to see financial success, and more importantly, financial freedom. Freedom to travel the world, freedom to better support your family, freedom to spend your time as you see fit rather than trading your life away for a nine-to-five.

You want to free yourself from whatever rut you find yourself in, because the only difference between a rut and a grave is the depth of the hole. This book is my way of sending a rope down to you so you can pull yourself out. Because success shouldn't be this grueling, life-long process, and it certainly doesn't have to be.

The best way to create success for yourself is to find someone who's already done it, figure out how they did it, and then copy that process (despite what you may have learned in school about the pitfalls of copying homework). These 7 secrets are my process for you to copy and follow in order to build your own success and generate your own 7 figures.

As you read this book, I recommend you have a highlighter. My goal is for this to be the most highlighted book in your library. Also have a journal and pen handy because there will be exercises and plenty of note-worthy content that you can use to apply in your life.

I firmly believe that significance comes more from what you give than what you receive. As you read these pages, be thinking of who you could bless by recommending they read it themselves.

Now go and see for yourself. Absorb the value and the knowledge between these pages and experience what happens when you choose to apply them in your life.

Enjoy unlocking the 7 *Secrets to Success!*

Chapter 1
The Key
To Winning

"You will never live life beyond your wildest expectations until you first have some wild expectations."

Picture this: It's ten years in the future and you're sitting in your home during the early evening. It's not a bad place by any means, but it's certainly no house of your dreams, either.

You think about work tomorrow and how your position, while it pays the bills, it makes you feel undervalued and underappreciated. In general, you feel like you're not being pushed in the kind of way that makes you grow, like you're not accessing the full potential of your abilities.

It's not that you hate your life or anything, but you're not exactly in love with it, either. You feel lukewarm and a bit tepid. You like to be grateful, and for the most part you do a pretty good job. Still, this nagging feeling creeps up into the back of your mind every now and then...

"I should be doing so much more with my life."

This is what happens if you choose to dream small. (And yes, it's always a choice.) When you have greatness within you, which you do, and you only come to meet that greatness halfway, you wind up having an okay life, even a "good" life, but not a great life, not an extraordinary life.

We've all seen the cheesy, overused quotes about shooting for the moon and landing among the stars or dreaming as if you'll live forever populating our social media feeds. But as predictable as they might sound, there's a powerful, irrefutable truth to them: big dreams matter.

One of the most important determinants for success across the board is the ability to think big and dream big dreams. Actors, artists, musicians, entrepreneurs, athletes, CEOs, writers—no matter the industry or niche they've mastered, all successful people have one thing in common: they got to where they are by first dreaming that they could.

One of the most widely accepted definitions of success is the progressive realization of a worthwhile *dream*. But before you can start progressing towards it, you must have a dream in the first place.

True success starts with your ability to first conceptualize your dream and then to believe wholeheartedly that its achievement is possible *for you*. When you allow yourself to define your dreams and then solidify your belief in their actualization, you create the space necessary for them to take root and bloom into reality.

In *Meditations*, the personal-journal-turned-best-selling-book of Roman Emperor Marcus Aurelius, he contends that "only big dreams have the power to move men's souls." It is this movement of soul that fosters desire, the fire necessary to fuel success.

Art Williams in his book *All You Can Do Is All You Can Do* states, and I agree, that the key to winning is desire.

Desire is the one element that will keep you going strong when things get tough. It's the one element that separates the good from the great, the mediocre from the truly successful, and it's what turns you from thinking that you *can't* to knowing that you *must*.

You can pursue a great education,
but you won't win without desire.

You can be blessed with a ton of talent,
but you won't win without desire.

You can rack up years of experience,
but you still won't win without desire.

Former football coach Vince Lombardi said it best with his famous quote, "Winning isn't everything, but *wanting* to win is." Desire is a foundational secret to success. But unfortunately, there's a narrative today that perpetuates this idea that desire is an innate trait that we are either born with or not. Like it's a genetic absolute in the same way as being born with green eyes or red hair.

I can't tell you how many times I've heard teachers, leaders, and business executives say things like, "Well, he just doesn't have the desire." Here's the reality: desire is something that *can* and *must* be created and harnessed from within. Remember this, you have to be disciplined in creating your desire.

We all have the same capacity for desire at birth, the same ability to generate that deeply burning flame. So why is it, then, that as we grow into adults some of us seem to have a flame that grows into a raging fire, while others' merely flicker weakly or, worse yet, get snuffed out entirely?

Like all fires that require oxygen and combustible material, desire must have life continually breathed into it and fuel to consistently burn.

What is the fuel that allows desire to turn into a blazing fire? *Dreams* are the fuel that fire desire.

If you want to harness your passion, your drive, your discipline, and your determination, you must have a burning desire. A burning desire requires dreams big enough to fuel it.

Ironically, one of the biggest issues people face when it comes to garnering success is actually quite small: the size of their dreams. For many, small dreams seem like a safer option. There's less risk involved because there's less of a chance the dream will fail—easy dreams are easy to obtain.

So this sense of ease leads people to set goals like getting out of debt or being able to pay all of their bills rather than setting goals like owning their own multi-million dollar home or having the freedom to live off of interest generated by their investments. They set low-level goals because society often dictates low-level thinking masqueraded as "safe" and "practical."

But this idea of safety, while comforting in theory, only serves to trap and confine us in reality. The hard truth is that small dreams produce small results. While this is a completely acceptable path for some, it will never be the path that leads to abundant success.

If you're the kind of person who is reading this book, you and I are kindred spirits because you're committed to playing a big game in this lifetime - small dreams just won't do.

In order to make a radical shift in your level of success, you first must make a radical shift in your thinking and break out of the mediocre mindset you've been trapped in.

While this may at first evoke a sense of fear, I urge you to not run from that and instead exploit it for your own gain. You see, I have this cardinal belief that, if utilized properly, *fear can be your best friend*. Fear can be one of the best internal motivators we have, our biological fight-or-flight response system that *urges us to fight*.

David J. Schwartz, a motivational writer and coach from the 50's, in his book *The Magic of Thinking Big* said that, "action cures fear" and that taking action in the direction of that fear will ultimately release you from it. But I will go one step further and add that *a discovered fear asks for action.*

To ignore that fear, to shy away from the thing that summons it, is to turn your back on the very thing that you are absolutely meant to do and to deny your purpose in life. If doing what it takes to achieve your dreams doesn't scare you at least a little bit, you're probably dreaming too small.

Unfortunately, fear isn't the only thing that holds people back from dreaming big. You might find yourself limiting your dreams out of guilt or shame, believing that your desire to become a millionaire is a selfish one. It's a story I've heard countless times and a self-limiting belief that far too many people share: that money is inherently evil and the desire for it somehow makes you a bad person.

Whatever the catalyst for this idea may be—an anti-materialistic parent, a political ideology, or a religious doctrine—trust me, I get it. For years, I used to get caught up feeling guilty about dreaming dreams that seemed overly materialistic. But when Warren Buffet donated billions of dollars to the Bill and Melinda Gates Foundation, an incredible private foundation servicing a myriad of philanthropic developments, I realized that through the accumulation of wealth, we are able to contribute to others in a way that would never be possible without it.

For many, achieving success may not be limited by guilt or shame, but by a mindset of scarcity. Many are plagued with the false belief that money is hard to come by.

If you've ever felt like it's only the lucky few who achieve millionaire status, let me enlighten you with some facts.

Credit Suisse put out their Global Wealth Report for 2019 affirming that there are over 22 million millionaires in the world. So my question to you is; if there are 22 million other people who have become a millionaire, why not you?

My firm belief, backed up by empirical evidence, is that there is an extreme abundance of wealth to be earned. There is literally no reason why you can't become a millionaire yourself if you're willing to simply follow the path that millionaires have charted before you. My coaching for you is to adopt that same belief and refuse to allow those diseased with a scarcity mindset steal that belief from you, as hard as they may try.

If it's possible for millions of people to become millionaires, which means it's also possible for you, why would you accept anything less?

As you read these words, begin to shift yourself out of the scarcity mindset. Accept the belief and have certainty that there is an abundance of wealth for you personally.

Know in your heart that the attainment of wealth, when done ethically, can and will contribute to and improve the quality of not only your own life, but society and the world as a whole.

Gaining financial security for yourself and your loved ones can have any number of positive consequences. At the personal level, the benefits of financial freedom can be seen immediately. It's not a stretch to argue that financial problems are the leading cause of stress in people's lives today; money issues cause more divorces, more prescriptions for anxiety medications, and more unhappiness than nearly anything else.

When the worry of money gets taken off your plate, you have the breathing room to be your best version of yourself. You have more time, energy, and mental focus to spend on the things that truly matter to you, like your family, children, or hobbies.

But your own life isn't the only one that can benefit from you seeing an increase in earnings. Maybe you have attained the level of success in your business that allows you to hire new employees and generate jobs, or the luxury of traveling the world and contributing to the economies of the various places you visit, or even allowing your spouse to quit their job and opening that position to someone new who can greatly benefit from that income. These are just small-scale examples of what personal financial security can do for the world around you.

What would it feel like if you had the means to improve the world on a larger scale? What if you gave yourself the opportunity to initiate, support, or aid in causes and missions you truly believed in—all because you were able to set fear aside, and accomplish things that others are too scared to dream of and strive for?

Doesn't that sound like an incredibly fulfilling, enriching, empowering position to be in? It can be yours, but only if you make the choice to dream big, and then go even further by taking action towards those dreams. It's only when you begin to realize that desiring wealth isn't wrong and can actually be applauded that you allow yourself to expand your thinking and shift your mindset, creating the mental space for big dreams to grow and flourish.

This also gives you the ability to let go of your need for wealth which, as contradictory as it might sound, is actually an important part of generating wealth. In fact, contribution is absolutely necessary. Think of the acquisition of wealth like the movement of water—old water has to flow out in order for new water to continuously flow in.

I'm not saying you shouldn't be smart with your money and save when it's applicable, but if you hoard your resources out of fear of what might happen if you were to lose them, that's living in scarcity—and living in scarcity has never helped anybody achieve big dreams.

At the end of the day, it isn't about the material possessions or even the wealth itself, it's about how you choose to use it in order to amplify the qualities of the type of person you want to become and the difference you make in the lives of others.

It's not only people's reluctance to dream big enough dreams, whether out of fear or guilt or both, that blocks their way forward on the path to success, but also their lack of faith in their own ability to achieve.

The other half of the equation is learning that dreams aren't contingent upon trying. Dreams are achieved through believing that it *will* happen with complete and total certainty.

If you want to achieve any goal, your first step is to declare it. Take one-hundred-percent responsibility for creating it, and then clear out all of the words like *hopefully*, *can't*, *maybe*, and the killer, *try*.

This is something that children have figured out much better than we have as adults. When you ask a child what they want to be or get in life, they don't respond with, "I'm going to *try* to be an astronaut" or "I'm going to *try* to be a fireman."

They don't assert that they will *try* for anything because they have no reason to believe that their dreams are not perfectly based in reality. They aren't hindered by the standard limitations that hold most adults back.

Children know and understand the power of dreaming big because they want to live a big life—their imagination is boundless and so, too, is their potential. And while the unlimited potential remains, the imagination begins to whittle away with each passing year.

Maybe it's society, maybe it's their teachers, maybe it's their parents, but somewhere along the way somebody tells them that they should be more realistic, that they should think more practically, that they should dream smaller. Someone convinces them that their dreams are unattainable, and so they grow into adults who think the same way. They turn from grown-ups into given-ups.

So whatever your dream might be, whatever aspirations you hold, I'm here to tell you that your chances of achieving them are going to drop drastically the moment you use the word *try*.

The second I hear someone say they're going to *try* to accomplish something, I immediately know that they're not going to do it.

Try is nothing more than a front-end excuse used when you have no commitment. Words like *try* are signs that you have no faith in your abilities and you're using your own power against yourself.

Dig deep and remember what it felt like as a child to be full of wonder and awe at all of the possibilities that stretched out before you. Unlearn the limited thinking imposed on you by all of the forces in the world trying to keep you and your dreams small and reignite the unwavering belief in yourself that you held when you were young.

Begin to imagine the most that's possible for your life. Begin to dream about the huge possibilities that are available for you to grab hold of. Begin to answer the question, "What would you attempt to do if you knew you could not fail?" and live as if that's the truth.

Recognize that you are like a plant—you grow in relation to the size of the container you are planted in. The bigger the pot, the bigger you'll get. Unlike a plant, however, *you* get to determine the size of your container.

Don't make the mistake of limiting your potential for growth by confining yourself to a pot that's too small because it feels "safe" and "realistic". That's how most people think, feel, and act throughout their lives, and that's why most people aren't successful or rich.

If you want to be above average, if you want to be one of the few that actually lives in order to make their dreams a reality, then you can't afford to think, feel, and act like most people. If you want to be above average, then you can't have average dreams.

You have to start thinking not just about what's possible, but what's *the most* that's possible. To be extraordinary, you have to dream extraordinary.

The good news is, you can start right now. I'm going to share with you something I've been doing for years that has consistently contributed to my success. If you are serious about achieving your dreams, then I urge you to do this immediately—before you put this book down, before you move on to the next chapter, before you do anything else, I want you to do this.

I want you to create a "Lifetime Dream List" of 100 things you want to be, do, have, learn and contribute in your lifetime... maybe even after you're gone.

Use the space below, or get out a journal and get your dreams out of your head and onto something concrete. When you write out your dreams and goals, you make a commitment to yourself that they are more than just ideas, that they *will be* your reality.

You breathe the first breath of life into them simply by acknowledging them in the real world and you take the first step towards making them come true.

To get you started, I'll give you an example of the first fifteen items I put on my list. These have changed over the years but this was the beginning of my list when I was twenty-four:

1. Red Dodge Viper Venom with the Hennessey package

2. 150-foot yacht with a helicopter landing pad, satellite communications systems, wave runners, and a ski boat

3. Yellow Lamborghini

4. Gulfstream Jet

5. Mountain home in Colorado with hot tub overlooking mountains, heated floors, glass walls on the side looking down the mountain, private lake on 15,000 acres of land

6. 15,000-square-foot home in the city with marble floors, dual staircases upon entry, three floors with theater that seats 50 people

7. Private secluded island with port for my yacht

8. Travel to 150 countries

9. Have close, personal friends on every continent

10. Become the founder of a charitable organization donating millions per year to charity

11. Become a bestselling author

12. Earn $1 million per year

13. Start a personal development school for children

14. See all 7 wonders of the world

15. Have six-pack abs

Over the years, this list has grown to over 300 items. I discipline myself to review this list regularly which is one of the reasons why I know I've now been able to check off over 100 of these bucket-list items.

I'll caution you… when I have people create this list in workshops, many people limit what they're willing to write down because of their addiction to being "realistic".

Here's the rule, if you want it, write it down whether you feel like it's possible or not.

When I wrote down "become a bestselling author", that was way more unrealistic in my mind than a gulfstream jet because, hell, I barely passed English in high school. I genuinely couldn't imagine writing a book, let alone it becoming a bestseller.

But the simple act of writing it down made it more real. As I grew as an entrepreneur and as a man, that goal started to become more real. Today I'm proud to say that not only have I authored or co-authored over 10 books that have become bestsellers, I've directly helped over 100 other people easily become bestselling authors through my publishing company.

Now it's your turn to dream wildly, to dream without limitations, to create a dream list that inspires you daily. Expand your thinking; there is no dream that is too big, too outlandish, too unrealistic, too selfish, too materialistic, too anything for this list.

Let go of your reservations and use this exercise to crystalize your wildest and most extravagant dreams. Keep going until you have at least 100 dreams written down! The sooner you do, the sooner you can start making those dreams a reality.

My Dream List:

1. _____
2. _____
3. _____
4. _____
5. _____
6. _____
7. _____
8. _____
9. _____
10. _____
11. _____
12. _____
13. _____
14. _____
15. _____
16. _____
17. _____
18. _____
19. _____
20. _____
21. _____
22. _____

30. _____
31. _____
32. _____
33. _____
34. _____
35. _____
36. _____
37. _____
38. _____
39. _____
40. _____
41. _____
42. _____
43. _____
44. _____
45. _____
46. _____
47. _____
48. _____
49. _____
50. _____
51. _____

23. _____
24. _____
25. _____
26. _____
27. _____
28. _____
29. _____
59. _____
60. _____
61. _____
62. _____
63. _____
64. _____
65. _____
66. _____
67. _____
68. _____
69. _____
70. _____
71. _____
72. _____
73. _____
74. _____
75. _____
76. _____
77. _____
78. _____
79. _____

52. _____
53. _____
54. _____
55. _____
56. _____
57. _____
58. _____
80. _____
81. _____
82. _____
83. _____
84. _____
85. _____
86. _____
87. _____
88. _____
89. _____
90. _____
91. _____
92. _____
93. _____
94. _____
95. _____
96. _____
97. _____
98. _____
99. _____
100. _____

Chapter 2

Becoming an Expert

"An investment in knowledge pays the best interest."
— Benjamin Franklin

What does it take to become the best? Here's a hint: it isn't talent.

One of the biggest misconceptions when it comes to success in any number of fields is the idea that you have to be innately gifted in order to reach the top or that you have to have been born with certain skills and talents necessary to outperform the rest of the competition.

If you remember in the introduction, I already laid the truth bare for you: I am not special. At least, not in any inherent way that gives me a natural advantage over anyone else.

So how exactly did I manage to become a millionaire in my twenties? It was understanding that, even though I wasn't naturally talented, I had just as much potential as anyone else.

While I knew I wasn't any more special than anyone else, I'll share with you a tactic that allowed me to be seen by others as amazingly talented, naturally gifted and viewed as head and shoulders above most others in my industry.

That "secret" strategy?

Become an expert.

In whatever field you're pursuing, whatever your business niche might be, whatever it is you're working towards that made you pick up and read this book in order to streamline your results, *make sure you are an expert in that field.*

Now I know what you're probably thinking... *"Become an expert? Doesn't that take years and years of discipline, study, time, and effort? I don't know if I can commit to that…"* Well, that's actually what I thought at first, too.

You can imagine my shock when I found out that it isn't only much, *much* easier to become an expert, it's actually one of the simplest things you can do, and one of the most beneficial ways you can use your precious time and energy.

How, you ask? The answer came to me late one night while I was on a teleseminar (any of you remember those?) and the highly successful multi-millionaire leading the seminar defined it like this:

"My definition of an expert is someone who is in the top one-percent knowledge level compared to everyone else in the world."

Again, you might be thinking to yourself, *"Matt, what in the world could possibly be simple about that? How can something like getting into the top one-percent of the entire world be so easy anyone can do it?"*

While it may appear to be an impossible task, just bear with me, because like I told you it's actually a pretty simple one to accomplish.

You're only five books away.

Don't worry, I'll give you a minute to finish rolling your eyes… but I promise I'm not joking.

Here's the reality. If you read just five books on any one subject, that's more than what 99% of everyone else will ever do. 99% of everyone else in your field will simply be too lazy to read five books on the subject.

So to be in the top one-percent knowledge level, you're just five books away. And just about anyone, including you, can dedicate themselves to reading just five books.

After speaking on stages to hundreds of thousands of network marketers in 35 countries across 6 continents, I've asked thousands of them; *"By a show of hands, how many of you have read five books specific to Network Marketing? Not sales books or personal development books, but five books written specifically on network marketing?"*

The response is always the same… at most, 2-3% of the room raise their hand. And these are the committed 10-20% of the people who are actually attending the trainings. 80-90% of network marketers never even attend events. So you can image, it's actually way less than 1% overall who have read 5 books specific to network marketing.

It's no surprise that the ones who do raise their hands, are typically the leaders making most of the money.

It sincerely boggles my mind that so many people will tell you they have these big goals and dreams of financial freedom, yet they won't commit to reading even five books on in the field they want to gain financial freedom from. It reminds me of the old saying, common sense is not so common.

When I understood that I could put myself in the top 1% knowledge level compared to everyone else in the world, I didn't commit to reading just 5 books. I was serious about becoming

SECRETS TO SUCCESS

a millionaire, so I read dozens of books specific to network marketing. In my library at home, I have a shelf dedicated to network marketing with over 80 books that I've read. Think that gives me a leg up on the competition? You better believe it.

I took the concept even further and listened to as many audio and video programs from top leaders that I could find. I may not have been a millionaire yet, but because I devoured so much information, my knowledge level got to the level of the million-dollar earners.

From there, because I also took massive action to apply the learnings, it was only a matter of time before my income caught up to my knowledge.

As my team started to grow, I quickly realized that one of the most critical elements to building a network marketing organization and sustaining growth, as is true with building any type of organization, is leadership.

So I decided to tackle becoming an expert in leadership next. I quickly read about 10 books on leadership feverishly taking notes as if I was going to be required to give a training on it afterward.

Important note: the last sentence is an accelerated learning strategy. Don't learn just for your own sake, learn for the sake of teaching it to others.

To put my leadership to the test, I started holding my own weekly training calls for my entire team and weekly live trainings for those on my team who had achieved certain levels of achievement.

Before each call or live event, I would review my notes and make highlights. Then I'd basically read through my notes and talk about how these principles applied to our business.

The results blew me away. Not only did I see increased levels of motivation on my team leading to increased production, people started telling me what an amazing leader I was. I even had people telling me that I was the greatest leader they had ever worked with.

28

It was pretty crazy because I was this 24-year-old kid who, honestly, felt pretty inferior and self-conscious. But because I was willing to simply go out and get the knowledge and then pass it on to my team with excitement and passion, I was lifted up to a level of leadership I didn't even feel I was worthy of. I ended up becoming the #1 earner in my company at 25 years old earning over $40,000 per month.

When I decided to start my first internet marketing company, I used the exact same process. I spent hours and hours reading eBooks and courses, listening to audios, and attending events... basically any and every piece of learning material that I could possibly get my hands on from people who had become millionaires through marketing online.

I was so committed and so convinced of my own ability to achieve my dreams, I didn't hesitate to invest heavily into my own knowledge. For two decades now, I've been a firm believer in Ben Franklin's famous quote:

"If you empty your wallet into your mind, your mind will fill up your wallet."

Unlike other types of investing, my mind and my knowledge is the *one thing that can never be taken from me*. To this day I continue to invest tens of thousands of dollars annually in my own learning in order to grow and maintain my wealth.

So what came from all of this knowledge? What did I have to show for all of my hard, diligent, dedicated work, my late nights and early mornings? What was the outcome of all of my mental blood, sweat, and tears? Nothing short of absolutely life-changing.

Not only did I become the #1 income earner in my company, my internet marketing company, which I ran on the side, generated $3.2 million in just over two years. Not bad for a guy who was living out of his car just a few years earlier at 21, huh?

Not only did following this strategy bring me greater financial freedom, it also created *massive confidence* in myself. One of the greatest gifts I've gained from mastering these seven strategies, is knowing with total certainty that I will never, ever, suffer from a lack of money. I hope you're starting to really get that wealth has nothing to do with any innate talents or skills.

In case you still don't believe me, the research backs it up—in 1985, Benjamin Bloom, a professor of Education at the University of Chicago, published a book pioneering the study of high performers and examining the critical factors that contribute to success in a skill.

He looked at 120 elite performers that had been internationally recognized for being the best of the best in their respective fields, from music and the arts, mathematics and neuroscience, to sports and physical superiority. Ultimately, his research concluded that there were no early indicators from their childhood that could have predicted their high level of future success.

What does that mean? Their childhood, the family they came from, their socioeconomic status, their gender, the schools they went to, virtually any factor you could think of was obsolete in determining whether or not they would achieve massive success.

Further research concludes that there isn't really a correlation between IQ and success in a multitude of fields, either. Consistently and conclusively, the research shows that *experts are made, not born, and that just anybody living can rise to the level of expert.*

If that's not enough, I'll give you some anecdotal evidence from a book I read years ago by John Paul Getty. In case you're not familiar with John Paul Getty, he was the richest man in the world in 1967, making his fortune by going all in on the oil business during the early 1900's.

If you've been paying attention, I bet you can guess one of the strategies Mr. Getty used to obtain his massive fortune. Unlike the majority of his competition, John Paul Getty never relied on randomly drilling for oil in hopes of striking the black gold that could catapult him to virtually limitless financial wealth. Instead, he decided to spend his time studying anything and everything he could get his hands on related to geology.

Because he dedicated his time and energy to becoming an expert on geology, he developed an expert level sense for where oil was most likely to be buried under the earth. Sure enough, he went on to become one of the most successful oil tycoons of all time.

If you find yourself wondering how you'll find the time to consume so much content—maybe you're already working a full-time job, maybe you have kids and a family to worry about, maybe balance is hard to find in life as it is—just think about how often we find ourselves driving or riding in the car, on a bus, walking some place, hell even using the toilet.

For most people, this is precious time wasted each and every day. Whether it's listening to music, talking on the phone, mindlessly scrolling through social media, or just sitting in silence waiting for the commute to be over, there are hours each week that could be dedicated to your learning.

A recent survey conducted by Valvoline found that the average American commute to work is roughly thirty-five minutes. That's over an hour a day in the car just going to and from work. Multiply that by five days a week and again by fifty-two weeks in a year, and that's over three-hundred hours spent in the car each year just for work alone. Factor in all of the other places we go and that's a lot of wasted time for the average person.

But the beautiful thing is that it doesn't have to be a waste of time, instead it can be your content consumption time, your Drive-Time University. Just imagine the number of books you could listen to, the podcast episodes you could tune in to, or the speaker presentations you could virtually attend if you had an extra three-hundred-plus hours each year!

I've managed to listen to thousands of hours of motivational and educational content over the years using this one small technique. It's allowed me to fuel my desire as well as my knowledge and to become an expert in many different areas. This is one of the best ways in which I've managed to drastically increase my learning, rapidly gain new levels of understanding and thus expertise, and see massive shifts in my success as a result.

Consuming content goes beyond aiding in your own knowledge and understanding though, it's also vital in creation, too. Whatever field you wish to increase your success in, whatever dream you're chasing that made you pick up this book, I would put money on it that some aspect of creation is involved.

It doesn't matter if you're looking to build your own business or brand, if you desire getting into writing, marketing or entrepreneurship, or whether you're in sales and looking to increase your numbers. No matter what your desire, there is some kind of creating you must do.

All great artists, whether they be artists in business or traditional arts, are inspired by other great artists and thinkers. They use the works that came before them as a basis for their own work, and then change and redefine it through their own style, taste, and technique.

All knowledge is learned, then transmuted, then applied, then learned again for another to continue the cycle. The success that people have experienced before you is not to be envied, *it is to be used* to achieve that same success for yourself and ultimately passed on to others.

My homework for you is to use the area below to choose at least three categories of expertise that will assist you in achieving your dreams, and then find at least five books in each of those areas for you to use to become an expert in.

To give you an example... let's say you want to become a millionaire in network marketing. You'll need to master the categories of:

1. Network marketing

2. Leadership
3. Communication Skills

You could also add the categories of mindset and sales.

If you want to be a millionaire in internet marketing, there are several sub-categories to internet marketing. Just a few might be:

1. Course creation
2. Social media marketing
3. Copywriting

If you need suggestions for books to read, I've listed a bunch of categories with book suggestions on my blog over at MattMorris. com/blog

Just go to that URL and in the search bar, type "top books" and you'll see a list of many different categories.

The thing about this secret is that it's incredibly simple to do, but it's also incredibly simple *not* to do. Making the list is simple. Following through and purchasing the books might deter you. Or maybe you've already got them on your shelf, but you haven't cracked any of them open yet. Or maybe yet, you've started the process but you're really sporadic and noncommittal in your reading of all five of them.

This is where separation between those who will achieve success and those who will not begins. Don't let laziness get in the way of your success. If you're committed to becoming an expert, you're only 5 books away.

The good news is that you've already started by reading this book. If mindset is one of the categories you desire to master, congratulations... when you've finished reading this book, you only have four more to go!

In the midst of consuming all of this information, so much of it can get lost if you don't take the time to process it before moving on to the next thing.

So how can you make sure that it doesn't? Take notes! It's as simple as what we all did back in high school. And before you let out a long and exhaustive groan, probably exactly like you did back then, let me tell you why this has been one of the most invaluable exercises I've ever done and continue to do to this day.

As I mentioned earlier, whenever you read a book or go through any type of course, take notes as if you'll be required to give a presentation or a training seminar on it the very next day. Even better, actually GIVE a training to someone the next day. Even if it's your spouse or even your child – when you train, you learn the information on an even deeper level.

Over the years, I've filled about 20 journals filled with knowledge. I consider these to be my Multi-Million Dollar Journals. Over the years these journals have been one of the most powerful reference guides that have elevated my expertise exponentially.

It's one of the reasons I was able to become a powerful speaker and trainer. At a moment's notice, I can give an hour-long training seminar on a variety of subjects because all I have to do is open my journal, pick a few pages to speak on, and the rest is cake.

So as you go out and hit up the bookstore or Amazon, make sure you take the time to grab a fresh notebook (or if you're one of those anti-paper tech lovers, open up a Word document or an Evernote specifically dedicated to this) and start creating your own Million-Dollar Journal.

By writing things down, not only are you reinforcing your ability to recall the information you've read through the act of writing (or typing) alone, but you also have a Cliff Notes version to refer back to anytime the information slips your mind.

Once you *are* an expert in any given field because you've taken the time to elevate your knowledge levels around it, the next step in garnering greater levels of success for yourself is to establish your credibility by becoming *known* as an expert in that field.

Let's be real, people like a name they can trust; and a name people can trust is more often than not synonymous with a name they know.

A strategy that catapulted my authority, expert status and ultimately my income, was to take my own knowledge and become an author. This is definitely an advanced strategy and isn't for everyone. But if you're the kind of person who has a sincere desire to become a thought leader and be perceived as a leader at the highest levels, it's definitely achievable.

As an author, you can use your book to brand yourself as an expert and use your book as the ultimate business card. You see it all the time: whether it's someone speaking on a podcast, being invited onto a talk show, or giving a speech at an event like TedX, the majority of people are introduced by their accolades—most commonly, being the author of a book.

Being an author immediately gives you huge levels of credibility and trust because most people see that and think, "Well she must be an expert, she's written a book!" You'll establish a higher level of respect than any competitor without that same status.

While we don't have time to go through the entire process of becoming an author – that would almost take an entire book in itself – just know that there are resources online that you can find that will help you through the process. After writing my first book over ten years ago, I can tell you the traditional process is a pretty grueling process.

Over the past few years, I've invested tens of thousands of dollars putting together the resources and a team to cut the process down from, on average, over a year to only 60 days or less. My publishing system has now helped hundreds of others become published authors. Many of them becoming bestselling authors.

If you'd like to know how you can become an author in the next 60 days, by investing less than 3 hours of your time, feel free to hop over to www.SuccessPublishing.com. It will open your mind up to how simple the process really is when you have the right team backing you up.

When asked how to get smarter, billionaire Warren Buffet replied, "Read five-hundred pages every week. That's how knowledge builds up, like compound interest."

All of you *can* do it, but I guarantee not many of you *will* do it. And while five-hundred pages a week is a great goal to strive for, it doesn't have to be your starting point in order to achieve that success he's talking about.

His point, and mine as well, is that if you want to be successful, you have to be willing to learn and to become an expert. By reading just five books on one particular subject, you'll drastically increase your knowledge level, you'll enhance your creative output capabilities, and you'll reach the level of expertise and gain the credibility necessary to set you apart from your competition and achieve higher levels of success because of it.

Let's get started laying out your expert roadmap below:

Category #1: _____

Books I'm committed to reading:

1. _____

2. _____

3. _____

4. _____

5. _____

Category #2: _____

Books I'm committed to reading:

1. _____
2. _____
3. _____
4. _____
5. _____

Category #3: _____

Books I'm committed to reading:

1. _____
2. _____
3. _____
4. _____
5. _____

Chapter 3
7 Figure Game Plan

"If you aim at nothing, you will hit it every time."
—Zig Ziglar

You know the age old saying, "If you fail to plan, you're planning to fail?" Rarely has someone achieved much success without a plan. They didn't just stumble upon it by accident or come across it blindly.

If you're reading this book, you've essentially raised your hand to say, "Yes! I want to become a millionaire."

But here's the cold hard truth.

Everyone WANTS to be a millionaire.

Most, however, will never achieve it.

I can determine with deadly accuracy if you're destined to become one of the "most" who will never achieve it, or if you're one of the few who have a real chance to become a millionaire, by asking you one simple question…

Do you have a *specific*, *detailed* and *actionable* GAME PLAN written down to become a millionaire?

So, my friend, do you?

If your answer is no, I'm sorry to say that your current destiny says you have almost zero chance of being a millionaire. That's the bad news.

The good news is, through reading this book, you can change your destiny starting today.

The reason I became a millionaire is because I had a plan to make that goal a reality. When I was in my early 20's, I set a goal and an action plan to become a millionaire by 30. For about 7 years I focused on it daily.

One simple strategy that allowed me to focus on this daily was setting my passwords on my computer screensaver and other websites and programs to "Millionaireby30". For 7 years I typed that every day, usually multiple times a day.

Looking back, I wish I had set it to "millionaireby27" and I probably would have achieved it then.

By setting that BHAG – Big Hairy Audacious Goal – and focusing on it daily, it eventually became a reality.

Before I get into the process, I'll share with you that I got derailed countless times.

- When I was 25, the company I was the #1 income earner for went out of business.

- When I was 26, my internet marketing company went $100,000 in debt and I had to claw my way out and ended up in a legal battle with my ex-business partner.

- When I was 27, the new network marketing company I became the top earner with made some terrible decisions that decimated the success of the company and caused me to leave.

A quote from an old poem comes to mind: "Sometimes the best laid plans of mice and men go awry." It is likely, okay even probable, that no matter what plan you set, you will get derailed.

Here's what you want to lock into your mind. It's a quote I heard from my good friend Troy Brown.

Plans change. Decisions don't.

The most important aspect of you becoming a millionaire is that it's a decision set in stone. If you look up the root word of decide – cide – just like genocide, suicide, pesticide, the dictionary gives you this definition: "denoting an act of killing".

When you truly DECIDE to become a millionaire, you "kill off" any other option.

If you're wishy washy about making a decision to become a millionaire, your results will be wishy washy as well. The only reason I was willing to continue striving for my commitment to become a millionaire, despite the incredible road-blocks, is because I killed off any other option. Becoming a millionaire wasn't just a wish, it was a must.

If you sincerely desire to become a millionaire, turn that desire into a decision and a commitment that you flat out refuse to accept anything less.

With that out of the way, let's talk about the anatomy of your game plan.

I like the phrase "game-plan" because I grew up playing sports, but you can call this process goal setting, goal getting, commitments, or whatever you'd like. To help you make this process easier, I'm going to boil down the 6 essential elements of a game plan.

1. You *must* be clear, concise, and **specific** with your goals.

2. You *must* be specific with the **time frame** you set in which to achieve those goals.

3. You *must* solidify your goals by **writing them down**.

4. You *must* determine a compelling **purpose** for why you want to achieve your goals.

5. You *must* develop a very simple and very specific **plan of action** that allows you to effectively achieve your goals.

6. You *must* think about your goals and **focus on your goals daily**.

This may seem elementary because you've likely seen this process before. The reason why I include it as one of the major strategies, and why I urge you not to tune out and skip this step, is because even though it's simple, it will be one of the most important conditions for you achieving millionaire status.

We tend to want to learn the fancy techniques but if you don't master the fundamentals, the advanced strategies will have little importance.

I'll tell you a quick story that illustrates the point.

When I was in 6th grade, I played football for The Cowboys in the youth football league in Lubbock, Texas when my mom was going to law school at Texas Tech. Our coach was amazingly smart. He had played football in college and was a real student of the game.

Outside of just the athletics of the game, we were taught discipline, integrity and the importance of hard work. He was also brilliant with strategy and seemed to know every play known to man. (at least in from my 6th grade perspective)

He taught us all kinds of advanced "trick" plays... double reverses, double passes, fake punts, fake snaps, on-side kicks, and others I can't even remember. We would spend hour upon hour attempting to master these trick plays and, as kids, we were super excited to learn them.

We were actually a force to be reckoned with. We won almost every game and made it to the playoffs. We won the first game or two and then had to play The Panthers. The Panthers were undefeated and, being a great coach, our coach scouted them out to learn their plan of attack.

When he prepped us for the big game, what was fascinating was that coach told us they were the most basic team he'd ever seen.

They ran only about 5 or 6 plays (we had dozens), no trick plays, and they never attempted a fake snap. If you don't know American football, that's when the offense tries to draw the defense offsides (making them draw a penalty) by not hiking the ball when the quarterback says "hut". Sometimes a quarterback will say hut 2, 3 or 4 times before the ball gets snapped. The Panthers quarterback just said "Ready, set, go" and they snapped the ball every time.

I played middle linebacker so I knew all I had to do was be ready for the 5 or 6 plays they would be running over and over. I remember wondering how the heck these guys could be undefeated being so basic.

That is, until the end of the first quarter when we were behind 21-0.

It was true that they ran only a few plays over and over. But DAMN if they didn't execute on them flawlessly every time. I had never been so frustrated in any game because I essentially KNEW what was coming, but because they were so strong, so fast, and blocked so perfectly, we just couldn't stop them.

The rest of the game didn't get much better. They crushed us and I've blocked the final score out of my memory.

You see, their coach had a completely different philosophy than ours. Rather than focusing on fancy tactics and tricks, he taught his team to obsessively focus on the basics much more than any other team in the league. We were what I would consider to be really "good" at dozens of plays while they had "mastery" of just a few.

The Panthers went on to win the youth league "Super Bowl". I ended up moving to Dallas after that season but if I had to guess, that coach went on to win many more Super Bowls with his team.

What I've found over my 24 years as an entrepreneur is much the same. Winning consistently isn't about chasing every new fancy tactic that comes along. I'll admit, I've been distracted by what I call "bright shiny object syndrome" too many times to count.

Sure, the basics of goal setting isn't sexy. But mark my words, what wins Super Bowl's in business is learning how to master and obsessively focus on the basics.

Now that you have the anatomy of goal setting with the 6 essential elements, let's talk about putting your goal into place.

If I were to let you take a peek inside my own personal goals, you might think it's a bit extreme. I have them broken down into each category of my life that's important to me.

I currently have 16 pages of goals broken out into the following categories:

- Family
- Relationship
- Fun & Personal
- Fitness
- Growth
- Giving
- Business
- Personal Brand
- Financial
- Investment

This is why I sometimes refer to my process as **Extreme Goal**

Setting!

Each category has its own page and some categories have multiple pages. Since I run more than one business, as an example, I have multiple business goals separated out.

While there are a ton of different ways you can structure your goals, I'll give you the process I've refined for myself over the past 15 years.

I break down each category into, usually a yearly goal, that gets reviewed every month. These goals are broken into 3 categories:

Section 1 – The Goal:

Lists a specific, well-defined goal *written in present tense* with a precise deadline by which to achieve that goal.

It may seem counter-intuitive to write a goal in present tense with a future date attached to it but stay with me and I'll explain in just a moment.

Section 2 – The Purpose:

This is where I define the purpose for my goal, and why it's an *absolute must* for me to achieve it. This is the driving force behind the goal and what motivates you from deep within.

Section 3 – The Action Plan:

Finally, this is where I break the goal down into its simplest form and create a step-by-step action plan that makes achieving that goal as efficient as it can possibly be.

Let's break these sections down a little bit further so you have complete clarity for your own extreme goal setting.

In section one, the keyword here is *specific*, and I want to make that very, *very* clear—like a sliding glass door you accidentally run into because it's so clean you don't even see it (it's okay, don't be embarrassed, we've all been there).

For example, let's say your goal is to earn a full-time income that allots you the means to not only cover all of your expenses, but gives you access to a high degree of flexibility, freedom, and an overall higher quality and enjoyment of life.

It isn't enough to simply write, "I will be earning a full-time income by next year" because one, it isn't using present-tense language and two, it's vague and leaves a lot to interpretation.

Let's talk about using present tense language first.

Every time you read your goal, which you should be doing daily, it makes an imprint into your subconscious mind. We'll be talking more about the subconscious later on in the book, but for now, just know that your subconscious mind is the driving force behind your results. This why we write our goals in the affirmative as if it's already true.

The issue with traditional goal setting is in the typical language which negatively programs your subconscious mind. Here's what I mean… when you say "I will be a millionaire on xyz date", every time you read it, you program your subconscious that you are not yet a millionaire.

Saying "I <u>will be</u> a millionaire" is essentially programming your subconscious mind that you are *not* a millionaire. This locks your subconscious into constantly thinking of what you don't have, which bring you more of that.

Instead, your goal should be written "I am a millionaire on xyz date".

Other examples:

- I am at 12% bodyfat on xyz date
- I have $100,000 saved in my bank account on xyz date

- I have 500 customers in my organization on xyz date
- I am happily married to my dream spouse on xyz date

Now, every time you read your goal, you are reading it as if it's already true. Sure, the date is in the future but for the key goal itself, you're positively programming your identity every time you read your goal.

Next, your goal must be specific. Vague goals will only lead to vague results.

If you set a goal saying "I am earning a full time income on xyz date", for all your subconscious mind knows, you could be a full-time income at the poverty level in your existing job.

Instead, write something along the lines of, "I *am* earning 'enter specific desire amount here' on 'insert exact date here' from my 'insert vehicle that allows you to generate the desired amount by the specified date here.'"

Maybe that looks something like, "I am earning $10,000 per month in December 2021 through my network marketing business."

What you're doing when you choose to get specific is imprinting that specific goal into your subconscious mind, literally reprogramming your entire reality as a result. It *has* to sink into your being on a subconscious level, because the subconscious is where all of the passion, drive, and creativity needed to achieve any one goal is born.

Once you've committed the effort to making your goal as straightforward and specific as possible, you can move onto section two.

This is your true motivator behind the goal – the core reason you're making an effort to pursue it at all.

Having a goal to achieve an income that brings you freedom in time, energy, location, and finances is great, but it *has* to go deeper than the dollar, otherwise you'll either feel overwhelmed by it all and let it drift away through inaction or you'll get burned out very quickly.

- *Why* do you want to achieve that level of wealth for yourself in the first place?
- What does enriching your quality and experience of life bring you that you don't already have?
- How does it help the people you love, and what does it do to bring greater value to the world in order to make it a better place for everyone?

While I'm not knocking the fact that chasing a high dollar amount or the rush of closing a big deal might be exciting for you, digging a little deeper and truly getting to the center of why you really want to be at that income level through your own business will awaken an entirely new level of drive and ambition within you. You must have a purpose that burns inside of you.

For whatever purpose comes to mind for each goal, keep asking yourself "why do I want that?" and keep digging by asking that question until you get to the most powerful answer for you.

Here are just a few examples to help you get an even clearer idea of what I mean by this:

"This goal IS my reality because I refuse to surrender the once-in-a-lifetime opportunity of seeing my children grow up because I made the choice to sacrifice my time, energy, and potential at a soul-sucking job building someone else's dream."

"This goal IS my reality because I know deep down that my one true calling in life is to be a mentor and role model for those who desire to escape a life of poverty, mediocrity, and limitation—and to settle for anything less would be emotional and spiritual suicide."

My blood is pumping just by writing those words down because they resonate so deeply. Both of those examples are certainly a *hell of a lot more motivating* than confining yourself to something as boring and as passionless as something like "I want to be rich."

If you truly desire to achieve at the highest levels, realize this isn't a dollars game. This is a purpose game. This is a "what kind of impact do you *really* want to make on the world with your one and only life?" game.

And the best of the best *live, breathe, and die* by that game.

When you create a compelling *why* behind each and every one of your goals, you'll create the motivation needed to accomplish it.

Now section three is where the rubber *really* meets the road—this is where you break your plan down step-by-step and into their simplest parts in order to achieve your goal.

To help you create your action plan, here are some questions you can ask yourself:

- What exactly must I do on a monthly basis to achieve this goal?

- What exactly must I do on a weekly basis to achieve this goal?

- What exactly must I do on a daily basis to achieve this goal?

- What must I learn to achieve this goal?

- How must I do to discipline myself to execute on this goal?

- Who do I need to motivate in order to achieve this goal?

- How do I ensure I manage my time most effectively to achieve this goal?

There are many others, but these are a few that I ask myself when I'm creating my action plan.

To help you out, here's an example of an action plan I created years ago for achieving one of my network marketing goals:

- I will personally sponsor at least 2 people per week into my business.

- I will attend at least one live guest presentations per week at our local meeting with at least 2 guests. In order to have 2 show up, I'll need to have 4-5 commit to coming.

- I will have at least 15 prospects per week watch our opportunity presentation online. (3 per day, 5 days per week)

- I will read and take notes for a minimum of 30 minutes per day from a book on leadership.

- I will call my mentor at least once per week.

- I will contact each and every person I've personally enrolled a minimum of 2 times per week in order to see how I might assist them in achieving their dreams.

- I will hold a weekly accountability and training session every Tuesday night after our guest presentation for my Managers and above. (That was a rank in my company) In this meeting, I will be personally accountable for my own production numbers.

- I will hold a Monday night leadership training at 9pm CST every week for my entire team.

- I will fly or drive to a different market twice per month to do a presentation and training.

- I will schedule out time in my planner every Sunday night blocking out times for inviting, events and learning.

If you're in network marketing, feel free to borrow or even steal these examples if they fit for your goals. But, of course, you'll want to tailor your action plan to whatever it is you're trying to accomplish for yourself.

For some goals, financial goals as an example, in my action plan, I will put space to list my income each month from January – December. This allows me to assess and make sure I'm on track to achieve my yearly goal.

For my learning goals, if I have a goal to read 26 books in a year, I'll list space for the 26 books and every time I read a book, I'll write it in the space created.

For personal branding goals, facebook engagement as an example, I'll list out my engagement score weekly to hold myself accountable.

Here's a few quick tips I use to keep myself accountable:

- Set a reminder in your phone for Sunday night at a certain time in order to set you weekly game plan.
- Set a reminder in your phone for the 1st day of the month to assess and revise your goals.
- Have an accountability partner you can report to on a weekly and monthly basis.

If you really want to maximize the process, consider how powerful something as simple as constantly keeping your goals within your awareness can be. Let me explain what I mean through an example from my own life almost 20 years ago.

I had been working as a waiter earning about $400 a week and had just moved out of my mom's house and could barely pay rent. I joined a network marketing company and was excited beyond belief to get myself out of my current situation.

I set my sights on the lofty goal of generating a weekly income of $2,000 per week within a 90-day period. Considering the fact that I had never earned that much per week, that was a pretty lofty goal.

But I knew there had been other people in network marketing get to that income level in that timeframe, so I knew it was at least a possibility if I was willing to get obsessively focused for a period of time.

To keep myself obsessively focused, I decided to create goal cards and put them everywhere so I would see, and focus on, that goal all day long.

I wrote out about a dozen index cards with a magic marker and wrote on each card:

I Am Earning $2,000 Per Week!

I placed those cards everywhere!

- In my car so I saw it every time I drove anywhere
- On the wall so it was the first thing you saw when you walked into my little one-bedroom apartment
- On the bar when you looked at my kitchen
- On the refrigerator
- On the microwave
- In the hallway
- On my desk
- On my computer
- On my bedroom door
- Above my bed
- On the bathroom mirror
- And even on the wall across from the toilet seat!

I got absolutely and totally **obsessed!**

Well, guess what happened?

Within 90 days I got to a $2,000 per week income. Now don't get me wrong. I'm not saying I achieved the goal solely because I focused on it. I'm not one of those airy-fairy trainers who believe the power of attraction can simply allow you to meditate and focus on your goals and they'll magically come to you.

I achieved that goal because I worked my ass off. Literally 80 hours a week, 6-7 days a week. I was non-stop and worked like a maniac.

When I achieved that goal, I took down all the index cards and replaced them with a new goal:

I Am Earning $10,000 Per Week!

I decided to keep pouring fuel on the fire and I continued

working like my life depended on it and 90 days after that, at the age of only 25, I achieved my goal of earning $10,000 per week!

Today, my life is well beyond that but I want to give you a major warning and have you learn from my mistakes.

There is a rule that says when you find something that works, keep doing it. I wish I would have taken that advice.

You see, when I achieved $10,000 per week, that was about 20 times what I was used to earning. It was beyond my realm of thinking to get to $25,000 per week and so I took down those goal cards and guess what I replace them with?

That's right – nothing.

I ended up staying stagnant for quite a while and my income even dropped for a period of time.

Looking back, if I knew what I know now, I would have replaced those goal card with "I Am Earning $25,000 Per Week!"

I eventually got my belief in alignment with my income and surpassed that $25,000 per week mark, but it took me a hell of a lot longer than it should have. This is one of the biggest reasons why you'll want to stay focused reading this book and pay close attention to the chapter on building your vision.

Despite many mistakes along the way, this extreme goal setting process has been, and continues to be, a major reason why my life continues to grow and flourish. When you have a clear path to achieve everything in life you desire, the likelihood of your achieving those desires goes up dramatically.

So stop right now and start putting your goals on paper. Get yourself crystal clear on:

1. What exactly you want
2. Why exactly you want it, and
3. Define a step-by-step game plan on achieving it

Create the map that will guide you towards your treasure and set sail on the open waters towards your personal version of success—who knows, you might find it much, much sooner than you think.

Chapter 4

Prerequisite of Massive Success

"The way to get started is to quit talking and begin doing"

—Walt Disney

You can read as many books as you'd like; you can listen to every podcast and attend every seminar related to your goals; you can have bigger dreams than anyone else, be the leading expert in your field, and have the most amazing game plan written out on paper, but that alone will get you *absolutely nowhere*.

I know, I know, I've been telling you all along that these are the secrets to generating the level of wealth you've always dreamed of, gaining financial freedom, and finally seeing the success you know you're capable of—but I'm also telling you that those steps in and of themselves are not enough.

So what, then, *does* it take to create massive success? Two words:

MASSIVE ACTION

What exactly does that mean? Well, let me explain by telling you a little story about the first time I truly achieved massive success in network marketing...

I had been in business for a while already, but with pretty limited success. Now at this point, I had already begun implementing some of the things I had learned along the way that I've shared with you: I had big dreams to become a top leader in the industry, fostered an immense amount of desire as a result of those dreams, started my journey towards expertise by consuming content put out by the people I considered to be greats, and thought I had laid out a pretty decent game plan—but I was still struggling.

I still hadn't managed to cross that threshold into massive success, and I knew that there was something 'more' that I hadn't quite grasped yet. Then I listened to a program by Jim Rohn that gave me the lightbulb moment that changed things for me.

What he explained is that if you want to experience the exact same level of success in network marketing as someone who has ten times your level of ability or experience, all you have to do is work ten times as hard.

At the time I heard this, my sponsor in the network marketing company I was involved in was as good as anyone I'd ever seen. He had earned over a million dollars in the industry and previously built an organization of over seventy-thousand people. On the scale of 1-10 he was a 10, no doubt.

I was working my job as a waiter in addition to my network marketing business. The best I had ever done in my five-year experience was to build a team of about 150 people with almost no duplication. That 150 wasn't even the active count but the total number of customers that had been enrolled in my organization, most of which spent less than $75 to join.

On a scale of 1-10, if he was a 10, I was at best a 3 or 4.

But Jim Rohn, unbeknownst to him, had planted a seed, an idea, that gave me hope and told me that I could outperform him and every other person in the company. All I had to do to outperform him was work 3-4 times as hard.

So what did I do? I did exactly what I teach the network marketing community *not* to do - I immediately quit my job. Now I know that sounds batshit crazy (and it was) but at 24 years old, I didn't have a lot to lose.

I was so determined to become the top earner in the company and realize my dreams, that I gave myself no other option. I would either go absolutely broke, or I would finally achieve the level of success that I was after. I intentionally put myself into what Chinese general and military strategist Sun Tzu, and later author Robert Greene, called **The Death Ground**.

In *The Art of War*, Sun Tzu defined it as such:

"When you have the enemy's strongholds on your rear, and narrow passes in front, it is hemmed-in ground. When there is no place of refuge at all, it is desperate ground."

Originally a strategy of warfare, the reasoning behind it is sound: an army backed up against a physical boundary, like a mountain or river, with no chance of escape and death viscerally present, will ultimately fight with double or even triple the resolve they would otherwise. It is the reaction to certain annihilation, it becomes a zero-sum outcome, it becomes kill or be killed.

"If you fight with all your might, there is a chance of life; where as death is certain if you stay in your corner." —The Art of War, Sun Tzu

So I backed myself into a corner, I burned the bridges behind me, and I made sure that I had absolutely no way to retreat.

It worked.

With no other option and no safety net to catch me, I made

a commitment to work like a madman and make damn sure I saw results. I started making phone calls non-stop, scheduling breakfast meetings at seven or eight in the morning every single day to show someone the presentation. When I wasn't presenting to someone one-on-one, I was on the phone prospecting.

I booked my calendar solid; giving a minimum of five presentations a day, making phone calls until eleven at night (because I knew that 11 PM in Texas was only 9 PM in California), and afterwards being so crazy I would put signs on the side of the road to generate leads three or four nights a week. Most days I didn't go to bed until 1 or 2 in the morning.

I worked over eighty hours a week, and within my first month in the business I personally enrolled 30 new people and became the top recruiter in the company. I've already alluded to this story earlier but within six weeks I was earning a full-time income of over a thousand dollars a week. At the ninety-day mark I was earning $2,000 a week. At the end of my first six months I was pulling in **$40,000** *a month*—that's more than a lot of people make in an *entire year*.

By drastically increasing the action I was willing to take, I managed to finally achieve the truly massive success I was after.

But that's not all that happened. During those first six months of going all in, I had worked more hours, gave more presentations, got on more phone calls, trained more people, and did more of everything than I had ever done in the entire lifetime that I had been in the industry.

Guess what happens when you do more of something on a more consistent basis? You get better at it. So not only was the action that I was taking increasing exponentially, but so was my level of skill.

After more than 20 years of studying success, I've boiled it down to a simple formula...

SUCCESS = FINANCIAL VEHICLE x SKILL x ACTION

Initially, my increase in action led to an increase in success. But as my action skyrocketed, my level of skill went through the roof right along with it and, you guessed it, that increased my success even further.

And the funny thing about this secret of massive action? It isn't a secret at all—every successful person in every single industry knows this. Need proof? Just take a look at all of the top athletes in the world.

Michael Phelps spent over twelve years training virtually nonstop to become the first person ever to win eight gold medals at a single Olympic Games; in fact, his coach Bob Bowman revealed during an interview that for five years straight Phelps didn't take a single day off, not even Christmas Day or his birthday.

Michael Jordan's Olympics teammate Steve Alford remarked that, "he was always the first one on the floor and the last one to leave."

In his book *Raise Your Game*, Alan Stein, Jr. reveals the principles of world-class athletic performers at the top of their game, the best of the best, and takes a look at what they've done to get there, then teaches how to apply those same principles to the business world.

Time and time again, the answer comes back to what he calls the "unseen hours"—the routines, rituals, and habits they establish and maintain every single day in order to achieve massive success.

All of the top performers in the world have that one thing in common: the absolute discipline and willingness to grind it out over and over again until the results manifest.

When speaking with Kobe Bryant, one of the best basketball players to ever live, Stein asked him why, if he was the best, was he was practicing the most basic drills. His answer?

"Why do you think I am the best in the world? I never get tired

of the basics."

Success comes down to your ability to stay disciplined and committed to simply doing the basics day in and day out over an extended period of time.

Sure, I quit my job and plunged head-first into unknown waters, putting myself on death ground and not allowing for retreat. But what that created was the space for the real massive action to take place. The eighty-hour work weeks, the constant pitching and getting rejected and pitching again. Going out and doing the work instead of sitting at home and relaxing.

Now, this is about the point where people often go on the defensive and shoot back with, *'Well, I just don't have the time.'*

If that's you right now, that's okay—I promise I'm not trying to shame you. But I am trying to keep you accountable and help you shift your thinking into a higher gear so that it doesn't have to be you anymore.

Think about the time spent throughout your day and be honest with yourself, how much of it is wasted?

For most people, the third most common use of time after sleeping and working is watching TV. On average? Two and a half to three hours—*a day*. Or maybe for you it's playing a game on your phone, listening to music for leisure, or scrolling pointlessly through social media. Whatever your vice, it's probably taking up way more of your time than you realize.

So why don't we utilize that spare time in our day to help further our goals and ambitions? Because too often we get fooled by our self-deceptions, genuinely believing there is no spare time at all when in reality what it comes down to is our priorities.

The next time you think you don't have time for something, be it the gym, working on your business, or anything else, ask yourself, 'How important is this to me?'

Instead of saying, 'I wish I could accomplish X goal today, but

I just don't have time,' what you're really saying is, 'I wish I could accomplish X goal today, but it just isn't important enough to me.'

Maybe thinking you don't have enough time isn't your problem. Maybe you've already committed to moving forward and you've got the ball rolling. You think you're doing all the right things, but you aren't seeing the results that you want and you can't figure out why.

This is the mistake that business coach James Clear outlines in his book *Atomic Habits*. It's the difference between being in **motion** and taking **action**. Now, maybe you're thinking, '*What the hell Matt, how is there a difference between action and motion? Don't they basically mean the same thing?*'

They *basically* do. But *basically* isn't the same as *is*. Being in motion is what a lot of the earlier chapters in this book touch on—when you're thinking, and dreaming, and planning, and strategizing, and learning, you're in motion. Those are all good and necessary things, but they'll never produce a result on their own. Taking action is doing anything that *actually moves the needle forward*.

When you're outlining what you'd like to accomplish in the next quarter of the year, you're in motion. When you're actually completing the tasks themselves, you're taking action.

When you're putting together your prospecting scripts, you're in motion. When you're actually calling prospects, you're taking action.

When you're researching effective social media marketing strategies for a digital product you want to put out, you're in motion. When you buy and run that Facebook ad for the product, you're taking action.

Being in motion has its place, but it will never produce the outcome you're looking for. Only taking action will.

So why do so many smart people get stuck in motion, and

struggle to take real action? Well, what blocks most people from most things?

Fear.

Fear of failure, fear of uncertainty, fear of looking stupid. You tell yourself you're finally ready to start doing the thing you've been avoiding for so long, but you aren't ready to fail at it yet.

Motion lets you feel like you're making progress and accomplishing things without running the risk of failure or criticism. But motion isn't progress, it's preparation for progress. When preparation turns into procrastination, something needs to change.

So how can you turn motion into action? There is no one simple answer to that question, but there are a lot of different strategies you can try implementing until you find what works best for you.

Obviously facing whatever fears you might be holding onto is the best place to start. For most of us, it's the fear of failure that keeps us from acting.

One strategy I've used that's worked well for facing that is simply shifting my mindset around the fear. Failure no longer scares me, it excites me. I don't mean that I'm out here purposely looking to fail at something, but failure has become a learning opportunity.

I've learned to be excited about learning how to do something differently, more effectively, better. When I fail at something, that means the next time I go out and try to do that thing, I'm a lot less likely to fall flat on my face.

Thomas Edison, one of the greatest inventors of all time, said, "I haven't failed. I've just found 10,000 ways that won't work." So don't be afraid to fail. The only way out is through, and the only way to get through is to start.

Another great way to move out of motion and into action is by giving yourself deadlines and holding them sacred. There's only so much learning, strategizing, and planning you can do once you've given yourself a time limit and commitment to sticking to it. This practice will allow you to develop a keen sense for balance between motion and action, and when it's time to move out of one and into the other.

Motion has its place, but only action will move you forward towards actually achieving the things you desire.

Here's an excellent exercise from the book *The Psychology Of Success* by Alison and David Price that you can follow as well to help get you excited about taking massive action.

Think about the goals you want to accomplish, the dreams you have, the aspirations you'd like to reach. Now picture this: You've worked today, and you're thinking about the things you'd like to do in order to make your dreams a reality. But your day was long and you're tired, so you come home and do nothing instead.

By the end of the week, you still haven't done anything. Life just got in the way and you never found the time. How do you feel about your goal?

It's now been over a month. You've maybe done some planning and researching, but little to no real progress has been made. How does that make you feel about yourself? What are you telling yourself? What are other people thinking about you?

A year later it's the same story. How do you feel about yourself and what you've been able to achieve? Are you happy with your life and the choices you've made?

Now rewind to present day. Although you were busy today, you made the decision to take a step, however big or small, towards achieving your goals. What is that step? How do you feel after it's completed?

Feeling energized by your progress, you continue to gain momentum throughout the week and take further action. How are you feeling about your goal?

By the end of the month, you're starting to reap the benefits of your hard work and you're seeing a lot of improvement towards your end goal. How does that make you feel about yourself? What are you telling yourself? What are other people thinking about you?

A year later, things are so different from how they used to be and you've come a long way. Think about all the things you've been able to achieve. How do you feel about yourself? Are you happy with your life and the choices you've made?

This is called thinking from the end, or visualizing what the end result of a series of choices will look like. It might seem hard to see the compounding effect of your daily choices five years down the line, but attempting to visualize that will give you a bigger picture of how the little things you do each day affect the reality that you experience in a massive way.

I heard a man speaking at a training seminar one day address the men in the audience, and what he said lit a fire in my belly. He told us:

"Men, if you're the kind of man that comes home after work, plops down on the couch in front of the television while you're barely making enough to pay the bills; if you're the kind of man that lets your favorite TV show or sports team be more important than your family's financial freedom; if you're the kind of man that's not willing to go out and fight for your success, fight for your family's success, and the kind of man who wants to leave a legacy of mediocrity for your children... I won't call you a loser, but you, my friend, are definitely not a winner."

I decided right then and there that I wasn't going to be that kind of man that could ever be referred to as a loser. I decided to make a commitment to not be a quitter. I decided that I would be man enough to take the rejection in stride, man enough to burn the candle at both ends, man enough to be able to provide financial security for my future family, and man enough to crawl through broken glass if that's what it took to achieve my dreams.

I want you to sit down and ask yourself these important questions:

1. Honestly, how committed am I to achieving my dreams and goals?

2. Sincerely, how hard am I willing to work to achieve my dreams and goals?

3. What will it feel like inside if I achieve my dreams and goals?

4. What will it feel like inside if let things like laziness, apathy, and fear cause my dreams and goals die inside of me?

Be introspective and honest with yourself as you ask these questions. The strongest reason you will (or won't) achieve your dreams are your emotions. It's why these questions are meant to elicit powerful emotions.

If you're willing to be honest, and emotional, with yourself, you'll be more willing to bring forth the emotions that will cause you to do what you must in order to make your dreams a reality.

In the end, you're going to be filled with one of two emotions:

- Immense Gratitude

  or

- Painful Regret

If your desire is to be filled with immense gratitude, it's going to require the discipline to lead yourself through the fear, through the hard work and through the countless obstacles that will most certainly get in your way.

Living the rest of your life with immense gratitude requires a choice.

It's simple actually – you choose to have discipline now or you choose to have regret later.

At this point you may be trying to squirm out and just put the decision off for another time. That procrastination is a choice... no choice at all is a choice for regret.

Here's how it will play out for you if you chose regret or if you simply lie to yourself and say you'll decide later.

It will sting a bit now because deep down, you know you're bigger than what's holding you back. You may lie to yourself that you're too young, too old, not enough experience, not good with people, don't have the education, too shy, or whatever else that comes up.

Listen, you can lie to yourself but you can't lie to me.

You have what it takes. You can't convince me otherwise. Having helped more than 50 people become million-dollar earners just within my own sales teams, there is no common background that made them earn a million dollars.

There are people less educated than you who did it, people older than you, younger than you, shyer than you, dumber than you and people who started out way more fearful than you.

How did they do it? They chose to have the discipline to overcome their challenges.

If it feels like I'm trying to get in your face and ruffle you feathers or maybe even piss you off, that's exactly what I'm trying to do.

I'm here to play a big game and to rise up leaders. I'm not here to try and make you feel good about the level of mediocrity you've been playing at thus far.

If you're honest, *you know you're capable of more.*

It's time.

It's time to step up and take your life to the next level.

The consequences of regret for you not stepping up are too big. Even though we may have never met, because you are my brother or sister, I love you too much to let you play small.

The regret you feel from not stepping up right now may not be devastating. It may only sting a bit right now. It stings because you know you're capable of more but you're letting your own bullshit get in the way.

The real consequences are years down the line. You see, regret isn't one of these things that just stings now and it's over.

Regret haunts you.

Regret haunts you five, ten, twenty years from now when you're still having to worry about money because you didn't step up.

Regret haunts you when five, ten, twenty years from now you still aren't driving the car you want or living in the home you want because you didn't step up.

Regret haunts you when you see other people taking the exotic vacations you could be taking but aren't because you refused to step up.

Regret haunts you when you see other people making a positive impact in the world and you're not because you refused to step up.

Regret haunts you when you look back at the people who doubted you and you know you made them right because you refused to step up.

I had those naysayers and doubters just like you may have had in your life. I had people laugh at me when I said I was going to be a millionaire. I had people tell me my business would never work.

But instead of letting their bullshit control me, or my own bullshit for that matter, I chose to step up.

Today, instead of them haunting me, I'm haunting them.

What's it going to be, my friend…

Are you going to be the haunted?

Or the haunter?

Chapter 5
Leadership Laws

"If you want to build a ship, don't drum up the men to gather wood, divide the work, and give orders. Instead, teach them to yearn for the vast and endless sea."

—Antoine de Saint-Exupery

By yourself, you may be the most talented, the most skilled, and the most educated person in the world, but the pinnacle of what you can ultimately accomplish is limited by what you can personally do and achieve every day.

Time is a finite and precious resource, and success is dependent on your ability to utilize what little you have effectively and efficiently. If you limit your success to your personal efforts, your achievements can only go as high as one person can reach.

It doesn't matter if you're currently reading this as a budding entrepreneur or an established veteran, the first thing you need to understand is that your capacity for scaling your business rises or falls in direct proportion to your capacity for exercising effective leadership.

As John Maxwell famously quotes, *"everything rises and falls on leadership."*

Governments, military organizations, corporations, churches, schools, and families will rise to success or plummet to failure based on the skills and abilities of its leader.

By no means do I claim to be the ultimate leader. If anything, I prefer to stay humble and give the credit away to others.

But along my journey over the past 24 years as an entrepreneur, I've been blessed to become the #1 income earner in three separate network marketing companies through building sales teams around the world.

I can't claim credit for it, but my organization has produced one of the fastest growing teams in the history of network marketing growing a customer base of over 1,000,000 in a seven year timeframe.

What's the secret?

I didn't do it alone.

I'd love to tell you it's because I'm this incredibly powerful and visionary leader who leads perfectly in every situation. But the truth is, I've succeeded despite myself.

I've succeeded despite a great number of personal shortcomings.

I've made just about every mistake in the book. Many of them, I've made multiple times. And when I say every mistake, I'm probably not far off.

I'm not ashamed to admit the huge mistakes I've made. Just a few are that I've:

- Blown countless people out by being too hard on them
- Been too soft on people and allowed them to take advantage of me and my company
- Sacrificed my integrity for the sake of profits
- Gone $30,000 in debt at 21

- Gotten my company $100,000 in debt at 26
- Gotten my company $750,000 in debt at 32
- Allowed my company to come crashing down and essentially go bankrupt because of bad decisions
- Sued others and been sued
- Blown major leaders out by spewing negativity

And the list could go on.

The reason why I say I'm not ashamed to admit my mistakes, is because if it weren't for the shortcomings and character flaws of my past, I would never have grown into the man I am today.

What I'm proud of, despite the failures, is that by simply making a lot of decisions and going for it, over and over and over, I always find any setbacks to be short lived.

Power doesn't come from pretending like you're perfect. Quite the opposite is true.

The most powerful person in the room is the person who has nothing to hide.

Many leaders parade around as if they've been this perfect bible thumping, tea totaling saint their entire life.

Well, if that's you, you probably won't relate much to me. But if, however, you're like the 99% of us who aren't Miss or Mister Perfect, my story should give you some hope.

Here's what I've discovered after 20+ years of leading men and women. What people want is transparency and vulnerability.

I don't try to make myself out to be perfect because by doing so, I do a terrible job of transferring belief. If people think you have to be perfect in order to be a successful leader, you fail massively in transferring belief because no one is perfect.

So, my friend, don't shy away from your mistakes. Your mistakes make you real and relatable. When you no longer have to hide from your imperfections, you gain the power to become unstoppable.

Another reason why I'm not ashamed to have made so many mistakes, is the simple fact that the entire reason why I've succeeded is actually *because* of those mistakes.

This is important… great leaders make lots of decisions. They may not always be the best decisions but the simple fact of making a lot of decisions trains you to learn how to make the right ones.

Because I have failed a lot, I have succeeded a lot.

Tom Watson, the founder of IBM once said, "If you want to dramatically increase your success, double your rate of failure."

Most people's lack of success isn't because they've failed, it's because they haven't failed enough.

If you've failed before, congratulations! That's the starting point for greatness.

If you're not willing to accept failure and move beyond it, you're not willing to be a great leader.

John Maxwell wrote an amazing book called failing forward. He masterfully explains how the successful use failure as invaluable learning lessons and how to use failure as stepping-stones toward your success.

We should not try to avoid failure at all costs. In fact, we should celebrate our failures because they've shown us what not to do.

The famed football coach Vince Lombardi was known for his amazing ability to motivate his players. When asked by a reporter what his key to success in motivating his players was, he said, "The key is knowing who to pat on the back and who to kick in the ass."

The reporter asked Mr. Lombardi "How do you know who to pat on the back and who to kick in the ass?"

My Lombardi replied, "Well, you pat the ones who need to be

kicked and you kick the ones who need to be patted long enough to figure out the difference."

If you're a student of success, it's most certain that you desire to become an amazing leader. The same was true for me throughout my entire journey. It's one of the topics I've studied more than anything else.

After over 20 years of leading teams that have produced over 50 million-dollar earners, thousands of people who've gotten to a full-time income as an entrepreneur, and well over $1 billion in sales, I've boiled down my leadership strategy into seven foundational principles.

These principles are absolutely non-negotiable. In fact, they are so important, I don't typically refer to them as leadership principles, but instead, leadership *laws*.

These are not recommendations, suggestions, or generalities; these are called *laws* for a reason—they must be implemented and followed one hundred percent of the time for sustained growth. As soon as you start to fall short on any of these principles, you start to see a fall in production.

Leadership Law #1: Have a dream larger than those you lead

"There is no passion to be found in playing small—in settling for a life that is less than the one you are capable of living." —Nelson Mandela

Big dreams are contagious. When you unapologetically and confidently live and breathe the desire for the achievement of a dream that seems impossible to those around you, it naturally lifts those people up and inspires them to join you in dreaming bigger than they had previously.

This is a prime example of emotional intelligence—the ability to transfer emotion to your organization—the key component to personal magnetism and a necessary quality for great leaders to have.

I see far too many aspiring and active leaders relying solely on their logical minds; focusing exclusively on what makes sense when it comes to the numbers and statistics, but paying little to no mind to what makes sense for the encouragement and well-being of the team that makes it possible for those numbers and statistics to continuously rise.

The greatest leaders are able to act effectively on what works best for both the logical and emotional aspects of their business, which keeps their profits and growth healthy while simultaneously keeping their team members enriched and feeling fulfilled in their efforts.

That's because people will not be inspired to act by the depth of your logic. They'll be moved and influenced by the height of your passion, your drive, your empathy, your dreams, and your vision.

People want a leader who will stir their blood, not appeal to their reason.

Consider for a moment that most people desire to be more than they are currently. They desire to lead bigger lives, to contribute and to live their lives in a more powerful way. Do you think it's much more likely they'll want to follow a leader who is passionate, excited and committed to achieving their dreams?

I heard this over 20 years ago and it's just as true today as it was back then…

When you get on fire, people will come from miles away to watch you burn.

When you open up to those around you, when you share your dreams and your passion and include them in the possibilities, you can't help but transfer that energy to them. You let them feel what you feel, and when they feel it, they realize it's a feeling they want to have more of, and they become excited and motivated by your passion.

They see you for who you are through your transparency and authenticity, allowing them the comfort they need to trust you— and the more they trust you, the more loyal and dedicated they'll be to help bring your vision to life.

The easiest way to say it is this…

Big dreamers inspire others to dream big dreams.

Life tends to beat us down and many suppress their dreams because of practicality and reason. When you share your dreams with excitement and passion, you give others permission to open up their own minds to dream again.

I already shared with you that the key to success is a massive desire and that dreams are the fuel that fire desire.

As a leader, you want to have an organization filled with other leaders who are bubbling over with desire for the accomplishment of their dreams. When you're bubbling over, you help to create that within your team.

To turn on their "dream machines", I'll often share my dream about buying my own 150-foot yacht to entertain my leaders. I'll talk about how we'll take the yacht island hopping for 2 or 3 weeks together. We'll have a full-time cook, server, and massage therapist onboard so we'll be very well taken care of. The yacht will have a helicopter and landing pad so we can take the helicopter over and explore the islands from the sky. We'll have a speed boat so we can go skiing and jet ski's that come down from the sides. We'll have a huge inflatable trampoline on the water with a massive people sized slingshot so we can launch ourselves into the water. There will also be a giant oversized hot tub where we'll spend evenings looking out at the stars as we cruise along popping bottles of Champaign.

I tell that dream with so much childlike enthusiasm that it

infects the crowd. I've had people retell the story to me from hearing it years earlier telling me how much it excited them.

Think about how you can tell your dream and paint a detailed picture full of life and color. Make the story come to life. Facts tell, but stories sell.

Here's an example for what I'm talking about. Take the same dream, presented two different ways...

"One day we'll be flying in our own corporate jet!"

Or

"Just think... soon we won't have to drive a car to the airport, show up an hour or two early just to make our flight, or be herded like cattle through the security check line. It'll be a limo picking us up and chauffeuring us to the secluded hanger, dropping us off right in front of our company jet where our private flight attendant will be waiting with champagne in hand. Hell, we won't even have to touch our bags —they'll be waiting for us as soon as we land, along with another limo to whisk us away all over again once we do."

Same exact message, but a stark difference in delivery. One might as well be a blank canvas, while the other is an artful piece that creates feelings of hope, excitement, and inspiration to act.

The more you and your followers are able to believe in living these dreams, the more concrete they'll become in your minds, leading you to create a reality worth experiencing. That's why, as the leader, it's your job to make sure that vision becomes clearer and clearer for both you and the people around you with each passing day.

Leadership Law #2: Always Have a Superior Attitude

"Courage is going from failure to failure without losing enthusiasm."
—Winston Churchill

76

I once heard a powerful leader say that fifty percent of success is attitude.

The other half?

Attitude.

A leader must have an **attitude** superior to those that you lead. Leaders fill themselves with positive thoughts and they act in an upbeat manner at all times when they're in front of those that they lead.

Positive attitudes are contagious, just like negative ones. But here's the thing, negative attitudes have an even greater affect and impact on your people.

It's your duty to always exemplify positivity to your team. Deal with your discouragement and dismay in private. If they visibly see you beginning to waver and lose face, how do you think they'll react? They'll begin to feel what you feel, and entire organizations can plummet as a result.

Negative emotions in a leader produce negative reactions in the team—so grin and bear what comes, and never let them see you sweat. This is the proverbial cross you must carry as a leader.

I don't tell you this out of theory, I tell you this out of experience because I've personally made this mistake and have had to bear the consequences.

A couple years ago, my company experienced some major challenges. One of my largest sales teams was led by another leader who was one of my very best friends.

One day he was sharing his frustrations and fears with me. Instead of showing him faith and determination like my mentor and company founder did with me, I verbally vomited all over him by sharing my own frustrations and fears. I thought since he was such a great friend, I could spew my negativity and it would be okay.

Not long after, he left the company and his organization plummeted. A tough lesson learned.

Always remember to keep your focus on the solutions to your problems rather than the problems themselves. Be the kind of leader that, when the storm comes (and it always does), you have the confidence, strength, and power of leadership to say, *"Bring it on!"*

Leadership Law #3: Commit to Integrity and Character

"Only a man's character is the real criterion of worth." —Eleanor Roosevelt

Nothing will burn down an organization or company faster than a leader that compromises their integrity for money. Long-term success can never come from lying, cheating, or stealing your way to the top. That kind of "success" (if you can even call it that) is always short lived because it erodes the one and only thing that matters most to aspiring leaders: trust.

Leaders who refuse to compromise their integrity inspire the kind of loyalty that will stay with them for decades.

Another critical aspect of integrity is the ability to be whole and undivided. It's being the same person in a packed-out room on stage as you are with your close friends and family.

Authenticity, especially in our modern world, is sacred. People, especially people playing at the highest levels, can sniff out a façade a mile away. Be true to your word and as you begin to rise as a powerful leader, you'll likely be tempted. Don't let the temptation for profits override your commitment to maintaining a strong character.

Another cardinal rule: never *ever* bad mouth someone within your organization behind their back. When someone hears you bad mouthing a colleague behind their back, that person will immediately wonder if you're bad mouthing them as well.

Keep your negativity to yourself. If criticism needs to be voiced, find a way to approach it tactfully and respectfully. If you have an issue with someone, go to that person directly to address it.

I've had to address major issues on numerous occasions with other leaders and I'll admit that it can be nerve wracking. It's easier to just sweep issues under the table and avoid confrontation. But what you'll find is that if you confront in a respectful manner, the person you are confronting will respect you more and you'll likely end up with an even stronger bond than you had before.

If you commit yourself to doing your best, to always doing the right thing even when it's difficult, your team will see that. As a result, confidence and faith in you will well up within them, which is exactly what will keep them around when the going gets tough. That's why no other principle is as effective or as crucial to maintaining leadership as integrity.

Leadership Law #4: Make a commitment to continued personal growth

Personal stagnation is the cause of decay and failure in most people's lives. In turn, it's the cause of decay and failure in most organizations.

A philosophy I learned early in my career is that "if you build people, you'll build a big business. If you don't build people, you'll never grow a big business."

The only reason... and I mean the ONLY reason, my organization produced over 1 million customers in my first 7 years is because our company has an extraordinary commitment to transforming lives through training events.

This is why I have to admit, I had little to do with producing one of the fastest growing organization in the history of network marketing.

Sure I may have personally sponsored over 300 people, traveled over 1 million miles supporting my teams, promoted these events like crazy and worked tremendously hard… but I never would have created this type of growth if it weren't for our commitment to creating a leadership development factory from our events.

I also have to make sure I'm growing myself in a huge way. While I certainly attended all the trainings myself, I also attended others, read voraciously and invested tens of thousands per year on my own personal growth.

This is critically important for you to know and always remember.

If you're not feeding yourself with growth, you can't feed your organization with growth. As the leader, it's your responsibility to stay ahead of your team when it comes to personal growth.

It might be nice to just sit back and train your team, but as a leader you have to stay out in front and constantly rise yourself to the next level.

The person who got you to where you are now, is not the same person who will get you to where you want to go.

No matter how high you rise on the leadership scale, you must always remain a student. If you're in network marketing, we are in the business of duplication. If you want your team to grow, you gotta grow!

Any success from a leader who lacks a commitment to personal growth will be temporary. I've seen so many people over the years have quick success only to see it fall down as fast as it went up.

These are the type of people who might have a ton of charisma, salesmanship, credibility, or a strong work ethic. They rocket through a few ranks producing like crazy and then, because they haven't worked on themselves, the hit upon what John Maxwell calls the law of the lid.

The law of the lid says that you will never grow beyond your level of leadership.

They hit a ceiling and because they haven't developed their internal strength of leadership, they get frustrated, sometimes sabotage their teams, and usually end up quitting. That is, unless they come to their senses and begin their journey to grow themselves from the inside out.

Don't let yourself fall victim to creating success only to have it come crumbling down.

If you want to build a really tall building, you have to dig a really deep foundation.

Start building your foundation now, and even on the way up as you're growing your empire, always keep digging the foundation deeper. The deeper your level of personal leadership and growth, the higher potential you'll have for growth.

Leadership Law #5: The Leader Sets the Bar - So Set the Bar High

"The quality of a person's life is in direct proportion to their commitment to excellence, regardless of their chosen field or endeavor." —Vince Lombardi

A manager is someone who tells others what to do so they can sit back and watch. A leader is someone who gets their hands dirty and sets the example for their team to follow.

Which one you choose to be will determine how quickly you're able to get ahead, because the work habits of the leader, good or bad, will inevitably be adopted by the organization.

In any organization, the leader determines psychologically

what level of productivity the rest of the organization is capable of collectively achieving. That's why you must set the bar as high as you possibly can, and then continuously work towards setting it even higher.

I shared with you in chapter four about how, when I was 24 years old, I personally sponsored 30 people in 30 days and ended up becoming the top in the company. Well, there's more to the story.

After sponsoring 30 people, I went into management mode. My team was exploding and it was all I could do to keep up with the demands of my team calling me for calls and meetings.

A few months in, I noticed an interesting thing. Even though I had a ton of people on my team who were better salespeople than me, had more credibility than me, and knew more people than me, not one single person had personally sponsored 30 people. Several had done more than 20, but none had done 30 or more.

I realized I had set the bar at 30.

So, I decided to take on a little experiment if you will. I made a commitment that, despite being so crazy busy, I would go out and sponsor 10 people in the next month.

I went into personal production mode again and actually spent less time supporting my team than I had been. I achieved my goal and got my total sponsored number up to 40.

Here's what was fascinating… within the next couple months, out of my entire team that had grown to hundreds of people, I had several who sponsored a total of 30 or more – but none who had achieved 40 or more. I simply raised the bar to 40 and it raised the production of the group.

Let this be one of the most important lessons for you as you become a powerful leader. It's up to us as the leader to show our team what's possible. True leaders lead by example.

Another incredible example of this principle is that of the world-class athlete Roger Bannister, and his success in breaking the four-minute mile. For years, it was assumed that a human being running a mile in under four minutes was physically impossible.

Hundreds of people tried getting below the mythical four-minute mark, but none were able to succeed. That was, of course, until Roger Bannister shocked the world by running a mile for the first time in recorded history in under four minutes.

Can you guess what happened next?

Within a short time of Roger breaking the record, someone else managed to do it as well. Then another, and another still. Today, thousands of others have run a mile in under four minutes.

The limitation was never a physical one, it was a psychological one, and Roger single handedly shattered it, shifting that mental paradigm, and making it possible for others to transcend in the same way he did.

Because they saw Roger succeed, they believed they could, too. That was enough for them to overcome their own self-imposed limitations.

Even though Roger may not have thought of himself as a leader, at least in the traditional sense, that's exactly what he was. He was someone that set a path for those with similar dreams and aspirations to follow.

Always remember, your team can see better than they hear!

True leadership is not a position or a title, true leadership is action and example.

Leadership Law #6: Your Team Will Do More for Recognition and Relationships Than They Will for the Money

Sure, we join a company to make money. But what keeps us in that company and motivates us to produce for that company, are the relationships and recognition we receive.

While it's not advisable to date a member on your team, I do encourage you to "date" your team in a non-romantic way. This is one of the greatest retention and relationship strategies that, admittedly, I'm nowhere near as good at as I used to be.

Think about this for a minute…

When you're dating or married, you (hopefully) do thoughtful things for your significant other to keep them happy and to make them feel respected and appreciated. These "acts of love" serve as a great relationship retention tool in keeping a relationship together.

At the time I'm writing this, we just had Valentine's day. On Valentine's Day, if you're doing what you're supposed to, you did some "acts of love" for your partner.

Maybe you:

- Got them a card with a sweet note
- Bought them gifts
- Took them to dinner
- Got them a massage
- Took them for a weekend getaway

Those are the things I did for my girl this past weekend because, well, I want to maintain a great relationship and make her feel loved and honored.

If you're smart, and believe me I'm no relationship guru, you don't only do these things on Valentine's day or special occasions. You do them just out the blue to let the person know you really care.

What if…

You took that same thoughtfulness and applied it to your organization?

What effect do you think it would have if you:

- Wrote personal cards to your team members when they achieved a significant milestone in their life or company promotion?
- Sent chocolates to every major leader in your group for Valentine's Day?
- Sent flowers to every female leader on Mother's Day?
- Sent books to your leaders for no reason at all?
- Mailed the leaders on your team a DVD copy of a movie that inspired you?
- Sent personalized Christmas gifts?

I can tell you firsthand, it makes them feel loved, honored and appreciated!

These are all things I've done for my leaders over my career and it's had a MASSIVE impact. When I owned my own network marketing company, this was my standard operating procedure. I had my assistant help coordinate these things for me.

It's one of the reasons why, despite having many major challenges, I never had one major leader leave my company in the 5 years I was in business.

Always remember this, people will do more for relationships than they will for the money. So make sure you're building relationship capital with your team.

You do that essentially by "dating" your team in a NON-romantic way.

Leadership Law #7: Persistence and Determination

"Press on. Nothing can take the place of persistence. Talent will not; the world is full of unsuccessful people with talent. Genius will not; unrewarded genius is almost a proverb. Education alone will not; the world is full of educated derelicts. Persistence and determination alone are omnipotent." —Calvin Coolidge

If you remember nothing else, remember that greatness takes time to achieve.

I was up to thirty-thousand dollars in debt and homeless in my first two to three years as an entrepreneur. But because I refused to give up and because I stuck to my guns despite my failures, I made it out of the seemingly endless tunnel of darkness and clawed my way into an amazing life that has exceeded my wildest dreams.

Because I chose to never give up, I haven't had to think about money in years because it hasn't been a concern to me for quite some time now. If I want to take my family for a weekend getaway out of the country, enjoy the comfort of a thousand-dollar per night hotel suite, or cut a big check to charity, I don't even have to think twice about it because it's such a low percentage of my income.

I don't tell you this to brag, I tell you this to show you that your efforts aren't in vain. Your sleepless nights and early mornings, your thoughts of, "Am I good enough? Am I just wasting my time? Is this really worth it?" are *not* in vein.

If you keep going, if you keep striving, and if you absolutely refuse to settle, your time will inevitably come. You may step up to the plate and strike out ninety-nine times but if you just keep swinging, eventually you'll smack a home run.

I'll admit, striking out for 5 years was a very long and painful process. I questioned myself a thousand times. I wanted to quit. It felt like I was banging my head against a wall and I was so filled up with frustration I couldn't sleep many nights.

A strategy that kept me going was, despite failing over and over, I decided to at least be proud of myself for continuing to press forward. As an entrepreneur and leader, you have to see failure as always being preferable to giving up on your dreams.

Successful people are successful because they do what the unsuccessful are unwilling to do. Winners are winners not because they never fail, but because they never give up.

A true leader will always find their way to the other side of the mountain, regardless of whether or not they have to climb it, go around it, or even go through it. They will do whatever it takes to overcome the challenges that arise. Know in your heart, there is always a way if you're willing to simply not give up.

In order to become a great leader, to hone your leadership skills, and to be the kind of person that others want to follow, you have to be introspective and honest about where you are versus where you want to be based on the Leadership Laws I've outlined in this chapter.

Break out a piece of paper, your phone, or your laptop and write down each of these 7 Laws of Leadership.

Then write down, on a scale of 1-10, how you rate yourself in each of the 7 laws.

For each law, write down what you feel you need to do in order to move yourself closer to a 10 for each law.

My friend, only you know the answer to that. Just know you already have a 10 inside you. It's just waiting to come out!

Chapter 6

Building Your Vision

*"The only limitations in your life are the
limiting beliefs in your mind."*
— Matt Morris

We typically think about vision as being something out into the future. A company vision, for example, is what a company wants to become or achieve out into the future.

You can think of a personal vision to be very similar.

The challenge most face in achieving a grand visionary future for themselves is the fact that it runs so completely contrary to their current vision, or identity, that's running them now.

Your current identity is made up of the beliefs you currently hold to be true about yourself. It's essentially how you genuinely see yourself.

Your personal identity subconsciously influences every decision you make, every action you take, and every action you don't take, thus influencing the level of success you're able to achieve.

Also, and this is important, the beliefs you have about other people, other things, and the world around you play a critical role in shaping your own identity.

Here's an example…

Because I grew up without much of it, I used to have a belief that money was hard to come by. I had a tremendous amount of scarcity when it came to money. Because of that, I had a very hard time seeing myself as someone who earned a lot of money.

If your personal identity is that of someone who is always struggling, then you will always find yourself struggling, even when you think you're working hard not to.

If your personal identity is that of someone who is out of shape or overweight, you may go on streaks where you eat right and exercise vigorously, but you tend to always shift right back into your old ways. Irresistible cravings, lethargy, sleeping in, etc. are somehow always overpowering your desire to be fit.

Why is that the case?

You'll want to write this down.

The Law of Commitment and Consistency.

Dr Cialdini, in his book Influence: The Psychology of Persuasion describes it as the way in which people want their beliefs and behaviors to be consistent with their values and self-image. Cialdini uses this law in relationship to persuasion and influence.

I would definitely recommend you read Cialdini's book to learn how to influence others, but I firmly believe the most important person we have to influence is our self. If you can't influence yourself in a powerful way, you'll have much less ability to influence anyone else.

Here's how I've used this law in relation to psychology for self-influence.

We'll start with my definition:

The law of commitment and consistency says that we will remain committed to remaining consistent with who we genuinely believe we are.

That being true, we must understand that in order to change our results, we have to change the beliefs we have about ourselves.

Let's take a deep dive into beliefs.

Take a look at the middle three letters of the word "beliefs" and what word do you see?

LIE

Consider for a moment that the story (the beliefs) you've been telling yourself about who you are as a person are simply lies you've made up.

Stories you may have accepted as "fact" like you're:

- Shy
- Self-conscious
- Lack self-confidence
- Not a morning person
- Afraid of public speaking
- Not a good communicator
- Not as smart as the others

Would it be empowering to know that any of the negative beliefs above, along with countless others, are nothing more than lies you created subconsciously through a belief building process you went through and didn't even knew you were going through it?

What makes me so certain these "character traits" are lies? Because I had all of those beliefs about myself that I once accepted as fact.

Today, if you told me I was any of those things, I would laugh

91

in your face because it would be completely absurd in my mind to accept any of those as true.

If you're willing to take a journey with me, I'll show you how I literally re-wrote my entire identity from a broke, scarcity filled, self-conscious young man, into a confident and powerful multi-millionaire.

I'm here to tell you that whatever limiting beliefs you've created for yourself are absolute and total crap. I'm proof of it and many of those I've mentored for the past 20 years are proof of it.

I don't know what lies you've accepted as fact for yourself but I know beyond a shadow of a doubt that, at your core, you are not a bad communicator, you are not unworthy of finding love, you are not a failure, you are not destined to always struggle, or any other negative belief.

Whatever they might be, you have the power to change those disempowering beliefs that serve only to limit the amount of success and personal fulfillment you experience.

If your current beliefs are what determine your success, the big question becomes how do you change your beliefs to create the results you want?

Before we answer that question, you first need to understand what shapes your beliefs in the first place. What has caused you to hold the beliefs that you do? Understanding where they came from will help you change them.

The belief building process you went through to come up with the beliefs you currently hold to be true, have been shaped by three main factors:

- Experiences
- External programming
- Internal programming

Experiences:

Every experience you've ever been through has been forever deposited and stored somewhere in your subconscious mind.

Maybe you were teased as a kid in school because you stuttered and now you believe you're a poor communicator. Maybe you were laughed at in class as a kid for giving the wrong answer and you took on a belief that you're not as smart as the other kids. Maybe you made a few horrible business choices when you were first starting out, and now you think you're lousy in business.

Whether you've realized it before now or not, those deposits were the first major factor that gave you the foundation of your identity.

Here's the way it works…

An event happens and then you make up a story (a belief) about what that event means.

Here's an example in my life.

My dad dropped me off at the library to do a book report when I was about 11. He told me to call him on the pay phone (back when we still had those) when I was finished and he'd come pick me up.

A couple hours later, I called and he didn't answer. I tried a few minutes later and no answer. I kept trying for the next hour until the library closed and he never answered. The library closed and there I was standing outside in the cold under on the patio of the library as it was pouring down rain.

We had recently moved to Charlotte, North Carolina and I wasn't 100% sure how to get home but I had a pretty good idea. I waited another 20 minutes or so and when it was apparent that dad wasn't coming, I ran home in the rain the 2 miles or so to our apartment.

When I walked in the apartment, dad was asleep on the couch with a bottle of scotch on the coffee table. He passed out drunk and couldn't hear the phone ring.

I still remember thinking how little he must love me to have forgotten about me.

You can see how this can carry out to develop an extremely negative belief. If my own father doesn't love me, why should I expect anyone else to love me. It wasn't hard for me to wire my brain to believe I wasn't lovable. It's no wonder I had such a hard time with girls for so many years. I never even imagined a pretty girl could like me.

So let's take a look at that example.

An event happened. Dad left me at the library.

I created a story that my dad didn't love me and I'm not lovable.

Now, was it really true that my dad didn't love me? Looking back on it now, not at all.

But at the time, that's what my eleven-year-old brain believed and accepted as fact.

Since I just made up the story about my dad not loving me, what would be a better story to make up?

What I choose to believe now is that my dad actually loved me very much. But was so diseased with alcoholism that no matter how much he loved anyone, he didn't have the power to control his demons.

Also, because he left me there it forced me to figure out my way home which made me independent at a very young age. Thank God he screwed up so much because had he not, I wouldn't be as independent and powerful of a leader as I am today.

Also, because my father, in so many cases, was such a bad example, I know exactly what NOT to do as a father to my three children.

When I created a different story about the event, it allowed me to create a positive story and actually be grateful for my father's mistake.

I have so many other examples from my childhood that shaped me into who I was as a young adult. Just like my library story, I've had to go through and re-define many of the negative beliefs I created and turn them into positives.

Think about some examples from your past. Can you think of some examples of events where you created a negative belief, but looking back now you can see it was really a blessing in disguise?

Real power comes from understanding that nothing has meaning until we give it meaning.

Events are neutral. It's the story we make up from the event that holds all the power.

This carries through in the business world all the time for entrepreneurs.

Most budding entrepreneurs experience failure in one form or another and, instead of realizing failure is simply part of the process, they adopt the belief that they *are* a failure and aren't cut out for entrepreneurialism.

What separates those who reach their potential and see massive success from those who don't has nothing to do with past failures. In fact, most successful entrepreneurs are successful because they were willing to fail over and over and simply not give up.

Start to see each failure as one step closer to success. Rather than whine, complain, and get depressed when things go wrong, *get excited* and use those as learning experiences and character-building exercises.

One of the most powerful examples of putting this concept into practice for me came when I started my first Internet marketing company. I launched the company with a good friend of mine who I had known for many years. After a few months of some serious struggle getting our technology built, we launched the company and saw some pretty phenomenal success quickly.

I was responsible for sales and marketing, while my partner handled the operations and the financial side of the business. Within a matter of months, we were generating almost a hundred thousand dollars per month. Life was great, and it seemed like we had the world in the palms of our hands.

This was greater success than either of us had ever experienced before and we were taking massive profits out on a weekly basis.

One day, I got a call from one of our vendors asking why he hadn't been paid in the last 60 days. Since I didn't handle the money, I had no idea this was happening and was totally confused. I went to my business partner and discovered that we had been spending more money than we were earning and were actually in debt.

It was in this moment that I discovered the significant philosophical differences between the two of us. I asserted that we absolutely needed to stop paying ourselves until the debt was paid off. He believed that we were the most important people in the equation and that we had to be paid first, before our vendors.

You can imagine my dilemma, realizing that I had been in partnership with someone who had an attitude that I believed would absolutely ruin our business reputation. After some heated arguments, he acquiesced and I thought all would be well.

I was scheduled to travel to Egypt for ten days and so, thinking the issue had been resolved, I left. But when I returned, our Director of Operations called me up and said, "Matt, we need to talk."

It turned out that the day I left, my partner, who had agreed to pay off our debts before paying anything to ourselves, took out two thousand dollars and then did it again a few days later.

I started looking through our bank records from the previous months and discovered that not only had he been using company funds to pay for his personal expenses to the tune of thousands of dollars, but we were also in debt much further than I thought. I was floored when I tallied it all up – we were $100,000 in debt!

I was furious, but even more than that I felt foolish. I felt so stupid for not taking responsibility for the financial side of things and for trusting someone else to do it.

I still remember having to lay off a couple of our employees. One of which was one of my best friends who worked in our customer service. He understood the situation and took it well and it didn't impact our friendship. But damn was it hard.

When he left the office, I went for a walk outside just circling the industrial complex we officed out of. I was so filled up with guilt asking myself, "How could you let this happen?" For a brief moment, because I had so much angst over having to let others down and lay them off, I sincerely questioned my ability to be a leader in business.

Thankfully, I understood this concept I'm going over with you and I realized I needed to create a better story based on the event that had just happened.

I said to myself, "Matt, because of this experience, it means that I'm a powerful businessman because now I know what not to do."

I chose to create a positive belief out of a negative experience.

This was a pivotal moment in my business career—because I chose a positive and empowering belief, I didn't give up. I took control of the company, I ended my partnership, I paid off all the debt, and our company went on to produce way more revenue than we ever had previously.

Your experiences in life will continue to shape your identity just as they have in the past. But the difference moving forward is that you now know that you have control over *how* they shape your identity.

You have the power to choose what belief, positive or negative, you will accept from each experience.

External Programming:

Whether you want to believe this or not, you've been programmed.

Your parents programmed you as a child to believe certain things about yourself, other people, money, religion, and many other things.

The school system, your friends, the media, television and other factors have programmed you to believe many of the things you do today.

Some of this programming has likely been healthy and gotten you to where you are and build you into the person you are today. Unfortunately, we also all have some less than empowering beliefs, and associated fears, that we've adopted as well from that external programing.

Babies have only 2 innate fears at birth; the fear of loud noises and the fear of falling. Most fear is learned; influenced by our environment and culture. A young child, for example, isn't naturally afraid of spiders but takes on that fear based on cues from parents or siblings.

By the time you were two years old, you heard the word no thousands of times more than you heard the word yes. It's no wonder so many people, when presented with an opportunity to start a business or take on a challenge, are paralyzed with fear and are hesitant to take action.

One of the most powerful ways that we shape our identity is based on the influence of others.

At some point in your life, you've most likely faced a moment where someone said something negative to you, or doubted your ability, without even meaning to. For a lot of people, that first comes from their parents and family members.

When I was in elementary school, in athletics class, we were told to run a one-mile race. While I had never been a super athlete, I definitely wasn't in bad shape either; I was just your average, skinny kid.

I gave the race my absolute all, and by the final lap I was right on the heels of the kid who was in first place, finishing just a couple of steps behind him. I was so ecstatic, and I remember running home that day after school to tell my mom about it because I was so proud.

When I told her, she was thrilled for me; she gave me a big hug and said something to the effect of, "Wow! That's great because our family aren't good runners at all."

I remember thinking to myself almost immediately that what I had done must have been a fluke since our family is bad at running. My mom wasn't even intending to say anything negative. It was just that, based on her experience and belief, our family didn't run very well.

But despite her innocent comment intended to make me feel good about myself, I took on the belief that I wasn't a good runner because my family isn't good at running. From that point forward, I never even tried to win a race.

Looking back at that now, it's evident that there was no basis for my inability to. In fact, based on experience of coming in second place out of 100 kids, it's obvious to me now that I was, actually, a good runner.

But because an authority figure made one simple throwaway statement, I took that on as a belief for myself and integrated it into my personal identity.

What's fascinating, and I could give several other examples from students I've coached, is that often our external program is even more powerful than the experiences we have. Which is why it's such an important warning to closely guard the ways in which you're being externally programmed.

The things that people say to you, whether they intentionally mean harm or not, can profoundly shape who you are—*but only if you let it*. You obviously can't go back into the past and change the negative things you've heard, but you can make the decision right now to no longer let those things define you.

You can recognize that what someone says about you has no basis in reality unless you *choose* to believe it. It's a choice. A choice you can start making right now, today, to say **no more**.

Beyond the choice to allow those things to influence your identity, you have the choice to severely restrict those disempowering statements at all.

Today, when someone says anything about me that is contrary to who I am or the person I want to become, I stand my ground in the face of that and simply say to them, "Please don't ever say that to me again."

When you set the ground rules for the way you want to be treated and spoken to, you show respect for yourself. When you show respect for yourself, people are more likely to follow suit and show respect for you in turn.

If someone continually disrespects you by saying disempowering things, you *must* find a way to separate yourself from that person, because their negative energy will only serve to hold you back.

This may be a cold way to look at it, but I've had to give this advice to kick some people in the ass to stop whining and allowing themselves to be talked down to. That advice is this:

If you allow someone to continually disrespect you, it's the same as disrespecting yourself.

Do not tolerate disrespect from anyone and especially not from yourself. You teach people how to treat you and if you don't teach them to treat you in a respectful and empowering way, that person doesn't deserve to be in your presence.

Surround yourself with people who lift you up, not those who pull you down.

Internal Programming

More than your experiences and more than the voices of the people around you, the greatest and most powerful way your beliefs are shaped is from your internal programming. Thankfully, it's also the mechanism you have the most control over.

Every word that comes out of your mouth and every thought that comes out of your mind serves as a programming tool. Those thoughts and words get entered into your subconscious mind and then work to create your habitual routines and mental thought patterns.

Those routines and patterns then influence the decisions you make and produce either a negative or a positive result. Here's the thing, most people think that the conscious mind is what rules your reality. Why wouldn't it be? Your conscious mind is the voice you hear. It's how you perceive the things around you and it's the vehicle through which you experience life.

But the reality is that your conscious mind is only the vehicle for perceiving and experiencing life. Your subconscious mind is the vehicle through which those perceptions and experiences are created in the first place.

Psychologists who study brain science agree that your subconscious mind is infinitely more powerful than your conscious mind. The subconscious is the driving force behind your belief system and your identity.

The subconscious mind has a goal which can serve you in a negative way or a positive way. That goal is to keep you in line with your identity. Remember the law of commitment and consistency?

If, based on your regular programming, you tell yourself you're broke, you're tired, and you suck as an entrepreneur, your subconscious mind figures out a way to keep you consistent with that programming.

If, however, you continually tell yourself you're wealthy, you're energized, and you're an amazing entrepreneur, your subconscious mind begins doing everything in its power to create *that* reality.

Here's the best way to understand it.

Whatever you say about yourself makes it more true.

- If you say, *"I'm an idiot."*, you become more of an idiot.
- If you say, *"I'm a genius."*, you become more of a genius.

Your consistent programing creates your identity.

The thoughts you think and focus on, and the words that come out of your mouth literally program your subconscious mind to strengthen your identity positively or negatively.

Here's the trick; your subconscious mind does not know the difference between the truth and a lie. It simply does its best to carry out exactly what you've programmed it to believe.

So when you say, "I'm sexy, I'm confident, I'm a millionaire," your conscious mind might be telling you you're full of it, but your subconscious mind, which is where the true power lies, will take that as a command and start working out a way for you to be all of those things.

The key to reprogramming your subconscious and change your deep seeded beliefs are to change your deposits. You do this by constantly filling your subconscious mind with empowering, uplifting, and motivating thoughts and words.

If you continually profess what you don't want, or focus on the things you don't have or aren't, then you actually attract more of that negativity and continue to reinforce more of that personal identity. **What you focus on expands**.

If you're anything like me, you've spent years negatively programming yourself to create a less than empowering identity.

I'll share with you my process.

Step 1 – Awareness

When I understood the power of the subconscious and how it's programmed, I started catching myself as I was negatively programming myself with things like, "I'm such an idiot, I have a terrible memory, there's just not enough time in the day, I hate mornings, I'm so broke" etc.

Step 2 – Reprogramming

When I caught myself saying, or thinking these things, I turned it around. So instead of saying "I'm such an idiot", I would say, "I'm such a genius".

"I have a terrible memory" became "I have an amazing memory".

"I'm so broke" became "I'm a millionaire".

If you've ever heard "fake it 'till you make it", I agree and disagree.

I disagree completely when it comes to "faking it" to the outside world. Never tell anyone else you're a millionaire if it's not true. You don't need to go into debt buying fancy watches and cars to make people think you're wealthier than you are, either.

Where I do agree is when it comes to faking it to yourself to program your subconscious mind.

I consider myself to be way more spiritual than religious, but I've studied much of the bible and love the scripture in Romans 4:17 that says, "Call those things which are not as though they were."

Step 3 – Create Your Ultimate Reality

This is where you're not just turning the negative programming into a positive, but instead you're consciously creating your own powerful identity.

This is your homework. It's called:

The Ultimate Version of You.

Break out a journal and write this:

If I could be anything in the world, I would be…

Then write down the most powerful version of you.

I'll share with you some of my process over the years.

When I first went through this process, I was in the phase of my networking career where I was a level 2 leader – a producer.

(If you're in network marketing, I'll be breaking down the 5 levels off leadership in my upcoming book on leadership.)

As a producer, I was able to sponsor people and make sales. I just couldn't get any duplication whatsoever.

I read a book by John Maxwell where he talked about the two types of math - addition and multiplication. He said when you recruit followers, you grow by addition. But when you recruit leaders, you grow by multiplication.

In network marketing, addition is slow and painful. Multiplication is fast and fun.

I was definitely in the slow and painful group.

I realized that the reason I couldn't seem to recruit leaders and was only recruiting followers, is because I was not showing up as a powerful leader myself.

I understood that for me to show up as a powerful leader, I needed to program my identity to become a powerful leader.

So I created an "I AM" programming statement. Here's what I came up with:

"I am the leader that every other leader wants to follow."

It felt like a complete lie when I said that to myself, but I realized if I wanted it to become true, I needed to program that as my reality. So I started saying it (only to myself) over and over every day. I used it as an affirmation every time I went into a presentation.

The more I said it, the more it felt natural. I started feeling more confident and powerful and it wasn't long before I was actually recruiting other leaders into my team which caused me to start growing by multiplication.

What I've been amazed with over the years is how quickly these programming affirmations have come to reality.

Here's one quick example which floored me when it happened.

I was speaking at Eric Worre's Go Pro event in Manchester, UK with about 2,000 attendees to close out the event.

Before I go on stage, I pray for God to speak through me and to produce the words that will make the biggest impact. After I say my prayer, I have speaker affirmations that I say to myself.

I *touch, move and inspire people, I motivate people to take action*, etc.

About 5 minutes before going on stage, as I'm thinking about the impact I wanted to make to the audience, I created a new affirmation that I said over and over before going on stage.

"I hit people right in the heart."

I got on stage and did my talk and felt like it went amazingly well. Afterwards, I came off stage to take pictures.

For the next 20 minutes or so, I took pictures and signed copies of my books. I noticed there was a lady standing off to the side just watching me.

After everyone was finished, she finally walked up to me and was clearly emotional. Her exact words which I'll never forget were, "I just wanted to tell you that at one point in your talk, I felt like a truck hit me right in my heart."

I immediately filled up with goosebumps because I had never said that affirmation "I hit people right in the heart" before and the very first time I said it, it manifested itself.

I could give you others that are equally mind blowing but just know that your programming will create your reality, sometimes in very short order.

So get to work, my friend.

Create 20 or more powerful I AM statements and affirmations for what you want the ultimate version of you to look like. Once you've created your list, come up with at least 10 that you will read aloud to yourself every day to program your identity.

It may feel awkward at first because your affirmations may seem so outlandish or unrealistic. But the more you say them, the more you program your subconscious to believe them. The more you believe them, the stronger your identity becomes. The stronger your identity becomes, the more powerful you are to manifest your dreams into reality.

"Watch your thoughts, they become your words. Watch your words, they become your actions. Watch your actions, they become your habits. Watch your habits, they become your character. Watch your character, it becomes your destiny." —Frank Outlaw

Chapter 7

The Quintessential
7-Figure Trait

*"There are two primary choices in life: to accept conditions as
they exist, or accept the responsibility for changing them."*
—Denis Waitley

There is no one secret to crossing that 7-figure threshold; it's
a culmination of excellence and effort across a multitude of
areas. You need to have wild expectations and dreams to turn
on a raging fire of desire. You'll need to gain the expertise and
specific knowledge for your chosen field of work. You'll need a
clear, concise game plan. You need to be willing to continuously
take massive action and accept failure as it comes. You need to
be able to take charge and inspire others to follow you. You need
to continue to grow your vision into the man or woman God
intended you to be.

If I look back on the key components that allowed me to become
a millionaire, there is one more I'd be remiss if I didn't share with
you. Along your journey to 7 figures and beyond, there are going
to be so many things that get in your way. So many obstacles that,

most, would use as an excuse for stopping them.

But you're not most.

If you're destined to achieve your greatest vision, you'll have to refrain from the most popular game in the world – the blame game.

Why is it the most popular game in the world? Because it's so much easier to blame someone or something else than to take ownership for your own lack of success.

If you truly want to step into a level of power that most will never realize, you'll adopt the 7th characteristic which is…

100% Responsibility

If you're able to recognize and freely accept that the quality of your life, good, bad, and everything in between, is your responsibility, then you have what it takes to create massive wealth, success, and freedom for yourself.

There is no conspiracy against you. The government is not responsible for your success. Your family and loved ones are not responsible for your success. No other person, company or entity of any kind is responsible for your success. Your success, or lack thereof, rests solely in your hands and your hands alone.

I can strike up a conversation with a complete stranger, and in less than five minutes I'll be able to accurately determine that person's potential for success is by asking them one simple question:

"What's your biggest failure in life?"

Their answer will tell me everything I need to know about whether they have what it takes to achieve high levels of success in their life. If they go on to tell me all about how someone else dropped the ball, or how their partner did them wrong, or how someone else got in the way, or XYZ circumstance wasn't "just right" and caused their failure, I know they have an extremely limited potential for success.

No matter what words of blame come out of their mouth, what they're really saying is, *"I have no power or control over the state of my own life."*

If you blame other people, circumstances, experiences, or *anything outside of you* for your life, then there is absolutely nothing I or anyone else can do to help you. You've already lost, *because you've made the choice to take yourself out as the primary mover in your own life.*

When you play the blame game, you're proclaiming to the world, *"Let me be powerless."*

The reason you have yet to achieve your dreams, the reason you haven't fulfilled your ambition, is because your level of personal responsibility hasn't yet reached the level needed in order to solidify your vision into reality.

If a jolt of anger, anxiety or fear just shot through your body and you're about ready to go on the defensive, it's okay.

Still to this day, I find myself playing the blame game. It's human nature. But because I know the principle of 100% responsibility and understand I'm powerless without it, I have to call bullshit on myself on a regular basis to correct my thinking.

When I step out of my power, I'm able to pretty quickly get myself back into it. While I'm by no means perfect, I'm certainly a thousand times better off now that I'm able to take ownership of my results.

Before I became a successful entrepreneur, before I became a thought leader, and before I was able to take charge and lead people around the world, I put the blame for my problems everywhere other than where it rightfully belonged—with me.

I would complain about things I didn't want to take ownership for. Like how the company website I was marketing for wasn't impressive enough, that the people I was enrolling weren't any good, that the systems we used weren't optimal. As far as I was concerned, all of these things, and any other thing I could use as a scapegoat to take the blame off of myself, were the reasons I was failing.

It had nothing to do with *me*, and everything to do with what was *outside of me*. As long as I was able to point my finger at someone or something else, as long as I was able to keep up the self-deception that I was this high performing superstar condemned to exist in a world where everything and everyone around me was flawed, my fragile little ego was content and satisfied.

And what do you think that mentality and behavior got me? Only more to complain about, more problems, and mediocre results.

The hard reality I eventually and inevitably had to face was that constantly shifting the blame and responsibility to someone or something else meant one thing: That I, Matt Morris, was a spineless little wimp. And as long as I stayed that way, I would never be deserving of true freedom—truly liberating, fulfilling, and massive success.

That's because powerful, strong, magnetic people are who they are because they own up to everything in their lives. They take one hundred percent responsibility for everything they have or don't have, feel or don't feel, attract or repel.

Whatever it is, they acknowledge their role in making it happen. Even when the experience they're having isn't their fault, they take it upon themselves to take responsibility for how the consequences impact them and their lives.

They don't make excuses like not having enough time in the day, or not having the energy, or 'insert basic, generic excuse we're all guilty of making at least a few times in our lives here.'

They embrace the fact that they are the primary mover of their fate, *making them the only one worthy of becoming masters of it.*

Do you think people like Bill Gates, Richard Branson, or Elon Musk whine about not having enough time in their absurdly busy and full days? Do you think they're constantly on the lookout with their heads on a swivel scouting out the next person or circumstance to blame for their problems and challenges? Absolutely not. They are where they are because they knew it was up to them to get it done. It was their 100% responsibility to make their lives worthwhile, to make something of themselves, to leave an impact and a legacy, and nobody else's.

Responsibility means response-ability; it is the power and the ability to choose how you will respond to the people, circumstances, and environment you find yourself surrounded by. When I learned this for myself, when I finally chose to embody and live by it, my life changed *substantially.*

Making this shift to 100% responsibility allowed me to stop creating excuses for why I couldn't and allowed me to create solutions for why I could.

If the company didn't have a good website or any sales tools or proper systems in place? Then I took the time and energy required in order to create my own.

If my sponsor wasn't able to get on the phone with me? I stopped whining and figured it out on my own.

If my team wasn't producing, I figured out ways to get them going or I created a new team.

In every instance, I put my focus toward the one and only variable within the equation I could truly control: myself. I stopped complaining about the cards I was dealt in any given situation and learned to play to the best of my ability with what I was given instead.

Here's a tip – play the hand you were dealt as if it's the exact hand you wanted.

If you want to change something, make something work, or achieve a goal, then declare it and take full responsibility for getting it done. Own it and embrace that you will find a way to accomplish it, whatever it takes.

Cut out all of the words that give you an out: hopefully, maybe, can't, and try. Do it or don't do it, but one way or another, take responsibility. Using weak, baseless language will always give you weak, baseless results and outcomes. Audacious, powerful goals need equally audacious and powerful language to match. Stop wasting your time making front-end excuses and committing halfway—stop giving up the power you have to direct your fate.

When you place the blame on other people or external circumstances, when you choose to use weak language like try or might, the only thing you're doing is hurting yourself.

In his book *Millionaire Success Habits*, successful businessman and entrepreneur Dean Graziosi tells a story and teaches a lesson that I'd like to share with you now. He says to imagine a farmer who gets up every day, throws grain on the back of his tractor, and drives out into the pasture to feed the cows, dumping the grain and heading back to the barn.

If he does this every single morning for ten, fifteen, twenty years, eventually he'll run ruts in the ground along the path to cows. Eventually, he'll get to the point where he could just get up, throw the grain on the back of his tractor, put it in gear, and let go of the wheel. The tractor will follow the ruts in the ground and take him right to the same spot he's been going to for years. His daily habits have created the conditions that could keep him going to the same spot over and over again.

For some people, they've become like the farmer; they have ruts that keep them doing the same thing over and over taking them down the same repeated path year after year. Often, they don't even realize that it was their own habits that created the ruts in the first place.

The important thing to remember about the farmer's story is this: to change the farmer's direction, to change his destiny, all he has to do is turn the wheel. It doesn't have to be some dramatic, 180-degree spin, with brakes squealing and mud flying everywhere; he just needs to turn it a little bit.

If you're ready to take control of your own destiny, you must take responsibility for the habits that have created your ruts and simply turn the wheel.

In this moment, I want you to make a promise to yourself. Promise that, from this day forward, you will hold yourself personally accountable—that you will take full responsibility for the state of your life and the choices you make for it.

Stop coming up with excuses and fooling yourself into believing that the person you are is anyone or anything else's fault but your own. Stop recklessly giving away your ambition, your vision, and your power to a refusal to look yourself in the mirror and take ownership and responsibility for your life.

Take 100% unwavering responsibility and not only will you reclaim your power, you will have gained the ability to control your destiny.

Final Thoughts

"Making a million dollars was one of the easiest things I've ever done. Believing it could happen to me was one of the hardest."

—Matt Morris

As a child, learning how to ride a bicycle can be a scary and frustrating experience.

I'm a father of three young children and teaching them how to ride brought back the memories when I was learning as a child myself.

Learning to steer and pedal without losing your balance can seem like the hardest, most impossible thing in the world. You get on. You fall over. You ride a little bit and fall over. The process repeats itself over and over until you finally get it.

But after you finally get it, and you find yourself riding smoothly and effortlessly down the sidewalk, it becomes second nature. You wonder how you thought simply getting up on the bike and riding ever seemed so hard.

Believe it or not, the same kind of thing tends to happen when you finally find yourself crossing that seven-figure threshold. Before getting there, you'll have all kinds of thoughts and feelings that tell you just how far away and difficult it all seems. But once you've actually done it, once you've actually learned how to get up and go, you'll find yourself asking, "Why did I ever think it seemed so out of reach?"

What I want you to know is that no matter how hard it may seem, no matter how scary or frustrating the process seems, you absolutely can do it.

If I look back 20 years ago to the person I was when I was intimidated and fearful, I realize today that I was way more powerful and capable than I thought I was at the time.

It's the same if I look back at myself 15 years ago, 10 years ago or even 5 years ago. I was way better than I thought I was. I just didn't realize the power I had inside me.

If I could fast-forward 10 years from today, I know if I looked back at myself right now, I'd know I was way more powerful than I think I am today.

And the same is true in your case.

Here's what I know about you… You are way better than you think you are.

You have a level of strength and leadership inside you now that is already immensely powerful. Please don't wait 20 years to realize it.

What I've come to realize in 25 years as an entrepreneur, helping so many thousands of people become full-time entrepreneurs, is that we all already have the power inside us to accomplish our goals and dreams.

Your biggest challenge is simply realizing your power and stepping into it.

My challenge to you is for you to step up as a powerful leader now. If you wait to step up until you have the results of a leader, I hate to break it to you, those results will never come.

Results come from becoming a leader now. Stepping into your power now. Assuming the role of a leader now.

The way transformation works is never Have – Do – Be.

Average thinking says once I have the results of a powerful leader, I'll do the things a powerful leader does, then I'll be a powerful leader.

Listen, the results of a powerful leader don't just magically appear. This mindset is the height of stupidity.

It's similar to people I've coached who are depressed and sad because they don't have their dream spouse. They walk around feeling down in the dumps because they think they need to have an amazing spouse to be happy.

But here's the likely truth – your dream spouse is probably someone who wants to be with someone who is *already* happy. So be happy now and it will allow you to attract your dream spouse.

The other mistaken belief is that it's a matter of Do – Have – Be.

This is the false thinking that says I will do a lot of work, then I'll have results, then I'll be a powerful leader. This is a formula for failure because the only way to create the results of a powerful leader is to do what a powerful leader does, and you can't do what a powerful leader does unless you ARE a powerful leader. You have to BE the powerful leader first.

The way transformation works is Be – Do – Have.

The great news is that you don't have to spend the next decade working your way up to being a leader. I'm about to tell you what my mentor told me approximately 20 years ago. Because I accepted this statement, it allowed me to step into a level of power I had never realized…

You are a leader when you decide to be.

In that moment, I just decided to *be* a leader and step into the role because here's the reality… No one is going to knight you a leader.

Leadership is not something you have to ask permission for. Leadership is not granted, it's assumed. You are who you say you are until you prove otherwise.

For you to become a powerful leader now, it's as simple as making the commitment to be a powerful leader and backing up that commitment with action. Don't overcomplicate this process. A powerful leader is already inside you so simply step into the role.

This allows you to do the things a powerful leader does and attract the people that powerful leaders attract.

In turn, you create the results and have what a powerful leader has.

Now don't get me wrong. It's not like you just step up as a leader, the seas part and you're a millionaire overnight.

It may not be easy. Achieving your dreams will most likely be a fight. It may be a huge struggle. You may lose sleep. It may require you to experience incredible levels of rejection.

In fact, it will probably hurt. But fighting for your destiny and fighting for your dreams is the one fight you will never regret.

You see, I believe you have a calling. Somewhere deep inside of you, a calling for your greatness is waiting to be answered. Maybe you have been ignoring it for years. You may have spent the last few years caught in your normal routine of just getting by, but nonetheless, your calling is there.

That calling is what begs of you to get out of the routine. Get out of the rut. Get out of mediocrity. The calling eats at you. It's the voice deep down in your gut that wants more.

It's that voice you hear when you want to take your family on an exotic vacation, but you can't afford it.

It's that voice you hear when you're at a restaurant and you have to look at the price before you look at the item to see if you can afford it.

It's the voice that you hear when you see someone else who is admired for doing great things in the world, and you realize you could do more.

You were not put on this earth for mediocrity. You were put on this earth to achieve your destiny. God has given you the power to achieve great heights, the power to make a difference in the world, and the power to realize your dreams.

My belief is that we were all given the exact same ability achieve success. How we manifest those abilities, however, is up to us.

Unfortunately, too many people live their lives filled with excuses. Excuses like, "I'm not smart enough, I don't have enough education, I'm too poor, I'm too old," or even the one I used for years, "I'm too young."

They're all lies that we use as excuses to live small, and whether you want to admit this about yourself or not, you were created with all the creativity, all the genius, all the determination, and all the strength that you need to create greatness in your life.

I believe everything happens for a reason and there are no coincidences. You didn't just pick this book up by some random chance or accident of fate. Out of the nearly eight billion people on this planet, this book found its way from my mind and into your hands for a purpose.

You have a purpose, a mission, a calling and you owe it to yourself and the world to answer that call. God has not only blessed you with the miracle of life, but also in the form of your unique gifts that only you are capable of sharing.

It's time to go share your unique gift to the world.

"Far better is it to dare mighty things, to win glorious triumphs, even though checkered by failure, than to take ranks with those poor spirits who neither enjoy much nor suffer much, because they live in the gray twilight of mediocrity that knows neither victory nor defeat."
—Theodore Roosevelt

Printed in Great Britain
by Amazon

67707611R00071